The Author

Renee Crosby is a Christian with spiritual gifts in teaching God's word. She is active in her home church and community. She has a desire to inspire and empower Christians, especially the laity, to realize that their modern faith walk can be so much more! She enjoys cooking and doing anything outdoors (except gardening). For some reason she can help people grow spiritually, but with plants? They don't have a fighting chance. She is currently working on her Master's degree in theology from Asbury Theological Seminary. She is married with one son and one daughter.

The Book

Soup Kitchen for the Soul combines testimony with a challenging scriptural foundation and follows it with specific guidance on how you can get out of your church and make a difference in your community. Each chapter builds on a Bible story and the author's personal experience, and ends with thought questions, and then action questions. References include specific ways in which you can take action on what you have been studying in the book.

This book is suitable for personal or small group study, or could be used effectively by an entire church to transform their ministry.

In the introduction Crosby says: "Upon entering Seminary, I was required to serve in the community and begrudgingly accepted my assignment, choosing to serve in a soup kitchen. While serving in the soup kitchen, God revealed himself to me in a profound and miraculous way. It was in restudying the scriptures with this new heart knowledge of God that allowed me to see a message of a mission for His people that we lack a connection with today. I began asking, 'What if ... What if I'm not the only one who doesn't understand the whole mission God has planned for us? What exactly are we supposed to be doing? Where in the Bible can we find directives on our missions for God? What if I wrote a book about radically new old ways of doing the gospel?'"

Soup Kitchen for the Soul is that book.

Soup Kitchen for the Soul
What I didn't learn about God in church, I learned in a soup kitchen!

by
Renee Crosby

Energion Publications
P. O. Box 841
Gonzalez, FL 32560
www.energionpubs.com

Energion Publications
P. O. Box 841
Gonzalez, FL 32560

Twenty percent of the royalties on this book go to Ft. Walton Beach Waterfront Rescue Mission.

Scripture quotations and references unless otherwise noted, are taken from the HOLY BIBLE, NEW INTERNATIONAL VERSION® Copyright © 1973, 1978, 1984 by International Bible Society. Used by permission of Zondervan Publishing House. All rights reserved.

Scripture quotations marked KJV are from the King James Version

Scripture quotations marked NLT are from *The Holy Bible*, New Living Translation copyright © 1996, 2004 by Tyndale House Foundation. Used by permission of Tyndale House Publishers, Inc., Carol Stream, Illinois 60188. All rights reserved.

Scripture quotations marked NKJV are from the New King James Version Copyright © 1982 by Thomas Nelson, Inc. Used by permission. All rights reserved.

Cover Design: Jason Neufeld, jasonneufelddesign.com
Cover Picture: Mickey C Photography,
                mickeycphotography.photoreflect.com
Hair and Make-up: Spoiled Gals Hair and Makeup LLC

ISBN10: 1-893729-79-6
ISBN13: 978-1-893729-79-7
Library of Congress Control Number: 2010929364

Copyright © 2010 by Renee J. Crosby, All Rights Reserved.

DEDICATION

To the place that removed the boulders on my way to Mount Zion, to the spirit and love found in my local soup kitchen that changed my life and my relationship with God and others…

the Ft. Walton Beach, FL
Waterfront Rescue Mission.

OWED TO JESUS

I owe my life to a wonderful friend of mine, Jesus that saved and healed a wretched soul as mine. I owe Him every blessing, every smile, every time my husband makes me blush, every time I smell my children's hair, every sunrise, every lady bug that makes me giggle, and every blessed tear in the pruning of my dead branches. I owe Him my gratitude, every inch of my heart and the deepest depths of my soul.

Foreword

In the first twenty-eight years of my Christian experience, I learned that each Christian had a spiritual gift that was to be used to serve the Body of Christ. I had finally figured out my spiritual gift of teaching and put it to good use in the church.

Upon entering Seminary, I was required to serve in the community and begrudgingly accepted my assignment and selected to serve in a soup kitchen. While serving in the soup kitchen, God revealed himself to me in a profound and miraculous way.

This new heart knowledge of God led me to reevaluate; to pray, read, and meditate on scriptures that allowed me to see a mission message for God's people—a message that today we lack a connection within our faith walk.

I began asking, "What if…".

What if... I'm not the only one who doesn't understand the whole mission God has planned for us? What exactly are we supposed to be doing? Where in the Bible can we find directives on our missions for God?

What if... I'm not the only one who had never contemplated where to meet God instead of being focused on God meeting me where I am?

What if... I'm not the only one who needed to go find God before I could find what it is I was really here for?

What if... I wrote a book about radically new-old ways of doing the gospel?

What if… we all had a 100% chance of getting to know God better?

What if... we all absolutely knew what God wants us to do and why and pursued it with conviction?

What if... I shared this message with other Christians?

What if... I could do some small part to change our mindset from being a come to me, God to being a go to God kind of Christian?

What if... we could get people to reconnect with our Christian heritage and the Godly design of our faith walk found in the Bible by getting refocused on feeding and serving others and not on self?

What if... Christians came to ask not what can God do for me today, but what can I do today for God and His kingdom?

That is the heart of a soup kitchen-like experience.

Table of Contents

Dedication... iii
Owed to Jesus.. iv
Forward.. v
Acknowledgments.. ix
Introduction... 1
1   My Story...3
2   What I didn't Learn about God in Church,
     I Learned in a Soup Kitchen.................................. 11
3   Defining Moments: The Christian Experience
     Revealed in the Passover Story...............................17
4   Defining Moments:
     The Christian Experience
     Revealed in the Crossing of the Red Sea Story............... 27
5   Reclaim The Promise:
     Stop Learning Faith; Start Doing Faith............................ 35
6   Reclaim the Promise:
     God's Design to Know Him...................................49
7   Defining Moments:
     We Are a Peculiar People Defined by Love..................... 65

8	Defining Moments:
	What Are We to "Do" Anyway?............................ 81
9	The Challenge.. 97
10	Awareness Training 113
	Bible Reading Study Guide................................ 123
	Scripture Index.. 127

Acknowledgments

Writing the book seemed easy compared to sitting down to write acknowledgments. I feel like its Oscar night, and I have sixty seconds to say thank you- and hope I don't forget to mention my spouse, my parents, my children, my friends, my in-laws, my brother, my brother in-law and my editor- of course! So, here is my attempt to document this abstract concept of gratitude to those that have helped me accomplish my first published works.

There is no published works without a publisher. So, thank you Energion Publications for taking a chance on a first time author like me! Your mission, your marketing plans, your grace and your company honor God! I feel privileged to work with you! The editing process surprisingly was less painful than child birth (I think that's a good thing?). The amount of professionalism, consistency, accuracy and sensitivity to presenting an authentic Godly message are some of your greatest strengths!

I can only hope to properly say thank you for the support of all my family and friends during this several year process to follow this desire to help spread this important message God has shared with me. A huge thank you to my wonderful husband and children that allowed me to nap during the day on a regular basis during the times when I wrote or edited in the middle of the night (when else would a stay at home mom write?).

It only seems fair to say much gratitude is sent out to those that have helped shaped me spiritually. There are many that have provided encouragement and molding in my own faith walk. They are the men and women in Bible studies I have sat with, cried with, and prayed with. They are the cherished brother and sister members of the "Out of the Box" Bible study group. They are the women that are paving the way as strong, Christian, grace-filled, female leaders for others to follow as an example who faithfully inspire me like Arthelene Rippy, Joyce Meyers, Beth Moore, Donna Partow, Lisa Bevere and others.

Then there are the kindnesses of strangers that have impacted this process as well. Thanks to Amy Newmark, editor with Chicken Soup for the Soul books for personally delivering the good news that my book title didn't infringe on Simon & Schuster's book titles. Thanks to the men & women I have encountered over the years at the Ft. Walton Beach Waterfront Rescue Mission that shared your stories, your pain and your victories about this mighty God we serve. You are the essence of hope in my life. You have been the face of Jesus to me. I am constantly inspired to proclaim the good news of how Jesus saves and Jesus loves, as boldly in faith as you do.

INTRODUCTION

I admit that I rarely read the introduction to any book. But now I have a better appreciation for the introduction as I write a preamble to my own book.

You need to have an understanding of where I'm coming from and where I'm going before you can appreciate the message God has placed on my heart.

Our God is a God of relationship, and I see this intro as establishing a relationship between me and each reader before we engage in intimate conversations about truly knowing God and His heart, and how that relates to the mission of His people.

It is with great honor that I write to you. I still chuckle when I think of how God uses me and my weaknesses for the good of God's kingdom. This book is to glorify Him.

I stand in awe of God's Word and the plans for us revealed through the Bible. God's Word and plans are amazing literary creations that have so many underlying themes and mysteries that I must remain careful to not present what has been revealed to me as having any authority over our Christian experience. I respectfully submit that this is God's story, yet my story within the context of the covenant relationship between God and me. It is how God connected and revealed truths to me about His nature, the scriptures and our mission while on earth through my relationship with Him while serving in a soup kitchen.

After a grace-filled period of time, I came to understand these truths and was given a desire to share them with others. May we all search out to experience God in radically new-old ways, however and wherever it is that God will choose to lead us to connect our modern faith walk with these scriptural truths.

God promises that if we stop limiting Him by requiring Him to meet us where we are, and instead we go and seek Him, that we will find Him!

In Deuteronomy 4:29, Moses reminds us to not make idols of any kind (which would include our self-centered nature to have God meet us where we are), "if from there you seek the LORD your God, you *will find him* if you *look for him* with all your heart and with all your soul."

When you decide to go and seek Him, He may lead you to your very own soup kitchen to serve and experience the applicability and meaningfulness of these scriptures in your life. Or He may choose to lead you to serve in a school as a mentor or in a court room as a *guardian ad litem* for a child , doing weekly laundry for the homeless, or packing sack lunches for the hungry.

Who knows where He will lead you to find Him when you respond to the promises and defining moments found in the scriptures? May these shared Christian moments allow you to see the message God placed upon my heart that allows you to reconnect with God and the missions set before His people in a radically new-old way.

1

My Story

Only as I sat down to reflect on my story for this book did I realize that my beginning relationship with Jesus was in a kitchen, yet long before my soup kitchen experience. It was in a little apartment in Indianapolis, Indiana. I was raised by a single mom and lived with her and my sister. We went to church and some classes on Sunday and knew about Jesus, but didn't really know Jesus.

My sister and I were embraced into a surrogate family that knew Jesus. Their family and our family became one. My mom worked days mostly, and my friend's parents worked nights, usually on weekends as musicians. So between the two households we were covered and together all the time at one house or the other, most often playing *Charlie's Angels*. We were the perfect representation of *Charlie's Angels*, the blonde, my sister, played Jill. My new found friend, turned sister, and the smart one, played Sabrina, while I was the other girl, stuck somewhere in the middle with no distinguishing label, and played Kelly.

Since "Sabrina's" parents had a flexible schedule during the week, they were always there for breakfast. We would spend endless breakfast mornings over at their house being fed scrambled eggs with green peppers, grits, toast and a good dose of vitamin pills to boot. Not only did this mom feed us breakfast, she would feed us with the love of Jesus. She was always on fire for the LORD. I remember her Bible being out and open and the sound of her flipping through pages as she would talk about this Jesus. Jesus was like another person at breakfast with us. Jesus this, Jesus that. I liked this guy Jesus. He was warm and inviting, kind, and full of hope.

It wasn't too long before I accepted Jesus as my Savior. I was in seventh grade. I think I had my own Bible at home, but it wasn't alive like hers. And even though I went to church to learn about Jesus, it was the Jesus that was in her kitchen that was alive to me. My real church was her kitchen, and my Bible was her Bible.

Only a few years later, they moved to the west coast. I stumbled in my faith walk for the next twenty or so years. I would hop from church to church, but never belonged to one. I had never gone to the lengths of an official membership at any of them.

Over the years, I gained ownership of a few more Bibles in different versions to help make more sense of my NKJV Bible, in which I had some simple phrases highlighted in red that I thought I understood, or heard God talking to me about.

Then, some twenty-two years later, I chose Jesus not only as my Savior, but as my LORD. I was baptized as an adult on August 13, 2001, at a lake submersion ceremony somewhere north of Tampa, FL. I was raised a new woman in Christ, went on my first date with my future husband four days later, and was married within five months. As a wedding gift from my mother-in-law, I received a new Bible with my new name inscribed on the outside, "Mrs. Renee J. Crosby".

Within the next two years I was indoctrinated into my first church membership through marriage. My husband was raised in and believed in belonging to a church. So we did church. I took my inscribed Bible to studies with some wonderful women, and started learning more about this Jesus fellow. This church became my church. This Body of Christ is what nurtured me, encouraged me and loved me. I had finally begun to understand the workings of Jesus and His Bride, the church.

The amount of exponential love and growth that I experienced in the Body of Christ was amazing. I can't imagine what my life would be like had I not been in that nest of the church. I know

My Story

for sure that it would have taken this bird a lot longer to learn how to fly had I not been there. Being in the Word of God set my heart on fire, and being connected within this Body of Christ healed me of my past and moved me into the future. Together they transformed me.

I had also come to understand that each member of the Body of Christ had spiritual gifts and work to do for the Kingdom of God with those gifts. Before long, I was serving in the church with my spiritual gifts.

The process to arrive at serving in my local church started with members encouraging me to teach adults the Word of God. I even thought I heard God calling me to teach. I wondered how this could be. God had started to knock on my door to serve in the local church.

After hearing about and having the opportunity to take a spiritual gift test, lo & behold, it confirmed that teaching was my strongest spiritual gift. Go figure! So, I moved forward with great discomfort towards my work for the Kingdom of God.

Why was I uncomfortable? Well, I couldn't believe that God could use me to help build up His Body of people. I couldn't believe that others in the Body of Christ saw gifts in me and asked me to serve in church. I couldn't believe that I had any amount of knowledge or wisdom or skill to actually teach the word of God. I was such a spiritual newbie.

I moved forward like a deer in headlights, eyes wide open yet blinded, not being able to see where to go. You see, I had Coach Christ in my corner of that wrestling ring. But, I was not the Christian athlete who jumped in the ring ready to take on my challenger. No sir. I was the scared, shivering, untrained first-timer who had to be shoved in the ring by the coach. Through many wrestling matches, I learned to trust Him that He had it all covered, whatever I was doing. I was to be the vessel. I wasn't in control.

One of those trust moments when God was working on me was the day before a women's conference where I was the key note speaker. I woke up at three in the morning on Friday, the day before the event, and Ephesians 6 was on my mind, the armor of God. I couldn't shake the feeling that God was leading me to this scripture, but I couldn't figure out why. I had planned to refer to it during my speaking engagement, but wasn't going in depth about it. What was God showing me?

I reviewed the scripture and my reference to it wondering if I had misused the reference, or my message about it was wrong (that shows my newbie insecurity). I meditated over the words, but wasn't hearing God lead me to expand the message on this scripture. I was perplexed. What was it about this scripture that God had placed it so heavily on my heart?

I was about to set it aside for a while, when I realized I had one more place to check. I went to the conference gift bags to check the handout with the scripture references. It was a five page document. Lo and behold, there it was. On the bottom of page four was item number forty-five, Ephesians 6:10-18, only it was split at the end of the page, and I had to go to the top of page five to finish reading it. The problem was that there was no page five, it was page four again. I had copied and stapled all of the scripture references with two page fours and didn't include page five–oops–leaving the Ephesians reference incomplete. I laughed. What an amazing God thing! I had no doubt that God had covered every last detail of the conference. All I had to do was trust Him, and allow Him to work through me.

That pivotal moment was a building block in the foundation of my trusting God and was a cornerstone in building my relationship with God. After that, my teaching started to change. I finally stopped using my notes in class as a crutch, and learned to let the Holy Spirit lead the class. Not that I didn't prepare for each class mind you. I learned that I didn't have to have all the answers, and that all I needed was a hungry heart for truth. God would provide the answers, the way, the knowledge and the wisdom.

About a year after the foundation was complete, another major point in my faith walk occurred; I was about to experience this fellow Jesus in a kitchen where he would really come alive for me. Only this time, my childhood kitchen spiritual mentor wouldn't be there with grits and vitamins. It was just me and Jesus.

After a couple of two by fours over the noggin, I finally heeded the call to start seminary. I was excited and nervous about taking my first class. In the first week, I was basically forced to choose to serve somewhere in our community for a semester long seminary project. I didn't want to serve, and was upset that I was required to do so.

My spiritual gifts were in teaching, and I was doing my part. I remember being on a church bus going to a leadership summit and talking to one of my pastors about how inappropriate, offensive, and annoying it was that I was being made to do such a thing. My gifts were to serve in the church, not out of the church. It seemed contrary to God's plan for me, and quite frankly a waste of my time.

You see, in the first twenty some years of my Christian experience, I had only come to understand that God's mission for us was to serve in the Body of Christ with our spiritual gifts. Somewhere in the context of my learning about being a Christian, I had equated serving in the Body of Christ to serving in the church (as in the church building/institution). I had taken several spiritual gifts tests and my gifts were to be used to teach the Body of Christ. The only spiritual gift from those tests that I could see that would require intentional work outside of the church walls was that of evangelism, which I found I didn't have, with great relief I might add. Can I get an Amen?

So, I thought we had it all covered. Why was I being required to serve in my community? Needless to say, I begrudgingly accepted the assignment and elected to serve in a soup kitchen. Have no doubt that the soup kitchen changed my life and my relationship with this wonderful friend of mine, Jesus.

Looking back, it seems ridiculous that I could have forgotten about my earliest kitchen experience where I learned of Jesus. I learned not just about Jesus, but this is where Jesus and the Bible came alive for me. My Jesus became my Savior at a kitchen table from a woman who was proclaiming the Good News and the vast benefits of vitamin consumption.

You may have guessed that by serving in my community at the Ft. Walton Beach Waterfront Rescue Mission that I learned that when Jesus talked about serving others, He wasn't just talking about our serving within the confines of our church walls. By serving outside of the church, I was introduced to many other faces of this mysterious and wondrous God and His mission for His people that cause us to rise up and taste mercy in the very soup we serve.

I had to ponder how I could have missed the mark so badly on what is required of me as a Christian to serve others as Jesus did–outside of the church walls. After the shock wore off, I realized I must not be the only one who thinks I am doing my part for the kingdom of God by serving in my church with my spiritual gifts. As I learned to articulate the vast amount of heartfelt knowledge God shared with me while serving in a soup kitchen I have come to do my part in some small way to realign God's people with the full mission God has set before us.

This book is about radically new-old ways of doing the gospel. It's about changing our mindset from being a "come to" church to becoming a "go from" church. The new-old way is about a dual approach to our Christian mission. It's about serving within the confines of our church walls, *and* about going and "bringing the Good News to the poor".

It's coming to understand and loving God in a more meaningful and relevant way because we have stopped limiting God and have gone to find Him where He is when we bring the Good News to the poor. That is where He reveals Himself to us in a personal, profound and miraculous way!

QUESTIONS FOR DISCUSSION

1. What key people have been influential in igniting or developing your faith walk? It could be several people from a teacher, or a parent, a neighbor, a friend's parent, a relative, a pastor or a co-worker.

2. Can you remember a time, place or event when and/or where this Jesus fellow "came alive" for you?

3. Describe the events surrounding the time when you accepted Jesus as your Savior. Was this the same time as when Jesus became your LORD, or did this develop later?

4. I ask that you challenge yourself to evaluate if you personally have come to expect God to meet you where you are, or have you experienced what it is like to go and seek God where He is?

5. What have you come to understand as the mission or missions God has for Christians? Do you believe we should use our spiritual gifts in the church (institution) and are you using them? What about this dual approach to our missions? Do you believe God desires and directs us all to also serve outside of the church walls?

2

What I Didn't Learn about God in Church, I Learned in a Soup Kitchen

In that soup kitchen, God revealed to me that I labor not in vain. God showed me a message, a mission for His people in which we lack a connection today. This message is to be shared so that we can learn and grow from it. What I hadn't yet learned about God in twenty-eight years of my faith walk since accepting Jesus as my Savior, I learned while serving only twenty-four cumulative hours (that's hours, not years) in a soup kitchen.

When I stepped out of my comfort zone in fear and apprehension and walked into that soup kitchen, my faith walk changed from being about having God meet me where I was to me meeting God where He was. The experience was a transforming miracle! It changed everything, and I mean everything.

It changed seeing with my eyes to seeing with my heart. It changed what I see, and where I see it. It changed my relationship with God, with my husband, my children and my friends. It changed my general demeanor with strangers from intimidating at times to always approachable. It changed my outlook, my tone of voice, my posture, my nature, my facial expressions, my wants, my goals, my love for others, my love for God and my soul. These are changes that you can experience too!

I write to inspire change in the way we do our Christianity and in the hope that we can all connect with God in a way that we all need but may not realize we do, as I didn't. It's about connecting with God in a radically new-old way outside of the church walls to see the scriptures come alive with meaning and relevance and power and truth.

Not only will Christians be able to experience God at a whole new level, but be inspired to engage in works for the Kingdom of God that have seemingly lost their significance in our modern faith walk. How or why part of our Christian works have lost significance isn't as important as to know who is behind the movement. It is solely the work of the enemy (who I will only refer to as "the enemy" because I don't believe he is worthy to even be mentioned by name). The enemy has worked toward having us forget some of the most astounding promises of God.

We are a sinful people, in a sinful world, constantly being bombarded with deceit and lies so deep that I cannot address them in this book. So our focus must be upon reclaiming some promises from God found in the scriptures. I can assure you these promises have not lost their relevance and can be reclaimed to enrich our modern faith walk!

As we awaken these sleeping promises in our souls, we will then come to evaluate what we can do better as we walk this Christian walk. Within my soup kitchen experience, it seems my soul was awakened, yet was in this groggy phase for a while. I was re-acclimating myself with my surroundings and this new heart vision I had, when I remember the moment my soul was awakened completely. While I was in the midst of awakening the experiences of the soup kitchen, one of my pastors asked a question of our

What I Didn't Learn about God in Church 13

congregation that snapped me to attention like that first sip of coffee in the morning.

He asked a very good question that has significant relevance for the life and purpose of the Body of Christ and our institutional churches. How we answer this question is a good barometer of determining whether we are doing a good job at the missions laid before us for a great and glorious God. The question was:

"What if the people of _____
(insert your church name here) **weren't here anymore? Would the community around you notice?"**

What a thought! Think about it. Would the community notice? If our answer is anything other than a resounding, absolute "Yes!", we have work to do.

Is your church and its people a real, tangible, visible reminder of an invisible God, besides the evidence of walls that make up the building? Are you a visible reminder of an invisible God? We, the Body of Christ, are to be a visible reminder of an invisible God to the world around us like the wedding ring is a visible reminder of an invisible love and commitment in a marriage.

The scriptural foundations of our Christian experience are carefully packed into a treasure chest that waits to be opened by us to find wonderful treasures inside. In order for us to do our Christianity in radically new-old ways, we must look for the treasures found within the precious stories and lessons given to us by the God-breathed word.

For about 15,372 hours, or the equivalent of 640 days, or 91 ½ weeks, or 21 months I prayed for the words to articulate the soul-inspiring experiences of the soup kitchen. I waited patiently (for once in my life) but with much anticipation, for God to reveal to me how to share those lessons. Finally, God answered my prayers.

One morning I woke up and the treasure chest was there. God had packed the most wonderful treasures inside to help me share the story of my soup kitchen experience. Within the treasure chest were two kinds of jewels that would allow me in some small way to help Christians live out a more fulfilling life as God had designed.

These radically new-old ways are found in the scriptures in the form of defining moments and reclaiming forgotten promises. These defining moments and forgotten promises are our legacy and heritage that we have somehow come to leave behind. Reconnecting with them will allow God to define our faith walk, not us.

The defining moments and forgotten promises found within this book will allow you to know God better. Once you experience these truths for yourself, you will come away with an increased amount of awe for God. These Biblical lessons result in a childlike wonder and awareness of how glorious our God is!

I hope by now that you are beginning to ask what it is that we have forgotten in our modern faith walk and how do we reclaim it. I also hope by now that you are beginning to wonder how to answer the questions of how do we function in this world for Christ, and where is our mandate to do so? Where in the Bible can we find directives on our missions for God? What exactly are we supposed to be doing?

How do we come to learn how to live our Christian lives, and is it as God intended? Is what we have learned about being a Christian correct? Is what we have learned about God correct? How do we know it's correct? Where are the answers? All of our answers can be found in the Bible. Within these pages that we'll share together I'm honored that you'll allow me to share with you my heart-changing experience in the soup kitchen in which God taught me about how to have a meaningful Christian walk beyond what I thought possible!

Ah, how did He teach me these things in the soup kitchen? I'm not sure I can fully explain that as it is the mysterious work of the Holy Spirit. I felt the truths first. I lived them. I experienced them in my heart, in my spirit. I didn't see the truths with my mind, but saw them with my heart. Then after the patient waiting, the pertinent scriptures for each of the key truths that I learned were revealed and fell clearly into one of two categories.

The first type of scriptural truths were revealed as promises that I either missed the meaning, or that I never claimed as my own. The other key truths that God revealed fell into the category of defining moments, or defining characteristics of living my Christian life as God designed. It is my desire to define or redefine the promises and identify the defining moments and characteristics of our faith walk that will lead to a more meaningful, relevant walk rooted in our Christian heritage and legacy. I will count on the Holy Spirit to make them yours.

One of the reasons I had not been moving in the world as God designed was because I didn't understand the way God designed us and our social structures and how we should function within them for Him. These are the truths I "hold to be self evident,"[1] and I hope you will come to see these truths as self evident when you go into the world to experience and claim these promises and defining moments.

I had to experience them first and then find the answers to the questions that I didn't even know I had. You on the other hand get to start by journeying with me into the Biblical truths that provide answers to questions we should all be asking, and then seek to experience them in the world by seeking out God.

I pray that these promises and defining moments come alive for you and speak to your spirit so that you can go and connect in the world as God designed. The result will be living a Christian life with authentic and truthful meaning and purpose, bringing great glory to God.

Let's pray before we begin our journey into the scriptures, shall we?

Dear God, you are an amazing God of grace and love with promises so concrete yet mysterious and profound that we

---

1 http://www.ushistory.org/declaration/document/index.htm

sometimes cannot comprehend with our human hearts and minds. We want to see these truths spoken to us spirit to spirit so that we can claim them with a hungry soul and a longing heart. We ban the enemy any access to our minds and hearts as we allow you to awaken our souls to reclaim sleeping promises. We pray that as we are awakened to radically new-old ways of experiencing and doing God in our world, through these truths revealed in the scriptures, that we will recommit ourselves to have, "Thy kingdom come, Thy will be done in earth as it is in heaven"(Matthew 6:10). Amen.

QUESTIONS FOR DISCUSSION

1. What if the people of _____ (insert your church name) weren't here anymore? Would the community around you notice?
2. Is our church a visible reminder of an invisible God besides the four walls that make up the building?
3. Are you a visible reminder of an invisible God?
4. If you were asked as a Christian what the purpose or meaning of life is, would you be able to give an answer, and what would your answer be at this point?
5. If you were asked what the missions of God's people were, would you be able to answer the question or know where in the scriptures to find the answers or refer someone to? If you can't do this yet–don't worry. Hopefully by the end of the book you will have a clear vision of our works for God and where to find our key missions laid out in the Bible.

3

Defining Moments: The Christian Experience Revealed in the Passover Story

When someone asks us why we are here, we need to fully know the answer. We need to understand what it is that God directs us to do. We need to understand where in the Bible to refer in order to gain an understanding of our mission. Ultimately, we need to evaluate and focus on seeking, finding, and living a life worthy of glory for God. We need to constantly re-evaluate how we are walking. Are we walking on the path God laid out for us, or have we gone off the path with a small wrong turn in the woods? Until we know what path we are to be walking on, how will we ever know we may have taken a wrong turn?

To help realign God's people with a fuller and more meaningful walk with God, I start with what I have come to see as two main building blocks that make up the foundation of our Christian experience. Our heritage, relationship and mission with God are established in the Passover and the Red Sea experiences. Every day I have been blessed as I review these two essential building blocks. I love to linger in the stories and their meaning.

These are the truths revealed to me in the soup kitchen that connect us with our basic path for Christian living. Within these two linked stories, God reveals a path for our Christian experience that is so relevant for us today, that it takes my breath away! Let us embark on the journey with one of our ancestors as they experience the Passover and the Red Sea first hand long ago.

THE STORY

My story goes back to my forefathers, the Israelites that came to fill the land of Egypt as foreigners. The sons of Jacob all came to live in Egypt through Joseph their brother. Joseph was a great Israelite who held a high position in Egypt during his day, second only in command to the Pharaoh himself. When Joseph was reunited with his family, they all moved to Egypt. But those days are long ago. Joseph and all of his brothers have passed on since then, but left a legacy of many descendants.

My ancestors may have been respected and worked in harmony with the Egyptians, but that is not so now. It is apparent how different we are today. The Egyptians are a people with deep cultural roots. They worship many gods and are great builders. You should see these pyramids that they built. But we on the other hand have the hearts of wanderers which is why many of my ancestors were shepherds, not builders. And though they worship many gods, we worship only one. We don't even really live among them as we reside in Goshen and they don't. This separation of ways and place only lends to more tension and disharmony. We have felt the strain of being foreigners here since we don't even have the rights of the native Egyptians in recent years, but it has gotten much worse.

This new Pharaoh that rules knows nothing of the days of teamwork between us and them. This king sees us only as a threat because there are so many of us. We heard rumblings that this Pharaoh thinks that since our numbers are so great we might organize against him and try to take over the kingdom. So, to remove that threat from his reign, he forced us into slavery to oppress us and kill our spirit and our growth. He not only stripped

The Passover Story

us of our freedom, but of our dignity. We are the underclass, the lowly, the hungry, the thirsty and the outcasts.

We feel defeated in so many ways. Our bodies are worn and ache from the long hours building with bricks and from lack of sleep. However, even in the midst of this suffering and torture, we are being blessed as God causes us to multiply and grow even stronger.

We live in times filled with fear, anger, horror, dread, anxiety and downright panic as the Pharaoh even ordered our own midwives to kill all of our baby boys being born. By the grace of God, the midwives stayed true to what was right and spared our Hebrew babies. Just when we thought our God spared us this horror, Pharaoh found out that the midwives disobeyed the orders. "Then Pharaoh gave this order to all his people: 'Every boy that is born you must throw into the Nile, but let every girl live'" (Exodus 1:22). A state sponsored campaign of genocide for God's chosen people, who would have thought?

Years have passed, but we are still under the yolk of slavery. We groan under the burden of slavery. Yet we cry out for help with pleas of deliverance to our God, the God of Abraham, Isaac, and Jacob our forefathers. We have faith in our God, for, "He administers justice for the fatherless and the widow, and loves the stranger, giving him food and clothing...for you were strangers in the land of Egypt" (Deuteronomy 10:18, 19b).

We know He hears our cries for help. It is later documented in the scriptures that this great God is about to execute a mighty work in saving His people. We are told that, "He looked down on the people of Israel and knew it was time to act, and acknowledged his obligation to help them," (Exodus 2:25) to deliver us from our oppression, our exploitation, our genocide.

In our need of deliverance, God has been preparing a man to lead us, Moses. Moses has come on our behalf to help us by mediating with Pharaoh, requesting that we be allowed to leave for three days to go and offer sacrifices to our God.

Pharaoh is not impressed with this God that we worship. He figures this God only wants to distract us from doing our work for the Pharaoh, and that we obviously had too much time on our hands to plan such things.

So Pharaoh responds with retaliation as we are now required to continue to build with bricks, but we now have to go and get the straw to make the bricks, and still have to meet the same building quota, which we know is impossible.

Some good Moses has done for us! We are angry at Moses. Perhaps we should have sent someone else to mediate with Pharaoh.

Moses then takes our grumblings and complaints to God, telling Him that this isn't working. We were hoping for some other plan to be given to Moses. But Moses comes back with the same plan. However, the LORD has sent Moses with more than the plan. He comes back to us with new promises from God, promises of our very own. These promises are our lifeline and we hold fast to them.

God has promised to free us, to redeem us, to make us His own special people. He will be our God. He promises we will know Him (Exodus 6:6-7).

Can you imagine that this great mighty God wants to know us and be in relationship with us? Our God promises to bring us into the land promised to our forefather, Joseph. We long for the day when He will give it to us as our own land (Exodus 6:8) . It almost seems unreal to us that we could come from our slavery and oppression to a land of our own flowing with milk and honey, but the hope of it keeps us going for now.

Even though we have been in Egypt for over four hundred years and pray for deliverance, little do we know that tonight, things will change in regards to our being released.

Moses has prepared us by telling us what God wants us to do regarding a new tradition of the Passover (Exodus 12:1-13). So we prepare for it by setting aside a lamb for slaughter, and now the time has come. Moses has told us to slaughter the lamb. We slaughter the lamb and drain the blood. Using hyssop branches, we dip them in blood and strike the top and sides of the door to mark our homes.

God has promised to do great and mighty things tonight. He will bring disaster on our oppressors, the Pharaoh and the land of Egypt, one more time. We have seen God bring about nine plagues in the land of Egypt already. "The court officials have even come to Pharaoh and appealed to him, 'How long will you let these disasters go on? Please let the Israelites go to serve the LORD their God! Don't you realize that Egypt lies in ruins?" (Exodus 10:7 NLT). Shockingly, the oppressor still won't let us go to worship the LORD.

Now we enter the safety of our homes, marked by blood stained door frames, and close the door. Tonight, it will be so peaceful, serene, and quiet that we won't even hear a dog bark. Yet the oppressor's land will be filled with terror, death, wailing and mourning as God kills all of Egypt's firstborn sons and firstborn male animals, while he will pass over our houses secured in the sacrificial blood on our door posts. "Then they will know that the Lord makes a distinction between the Egyptians and the Israelites" (Exodus 11:7b).

Tonight we will come to experience a peace like we have never known. This peace God will grant us is part of the promise to redeem us. Tonight, this peace will redeem our dignity. This peace will liberate us. This peace showers us with the love of our great God. This peace blankets us with God's presence, and makes us feel how special we are to him. He is our hope. God is doing our justice work for us. He hasn't forgotten us lowly, tired, oppressed slaves. He is working for us against evil and injustice.

As we sit to eat our meal of roast lamb with bitter herbs and bread without yeast, we wear our traveling clothes and our sandals.

We have our walking sticks with us, and we eat quickly. God has asked that we do this as if prepared for a long journey. Little do we know that soon we will be gathering our kneading bowls, and will be receiving many goods from the Egyptians.

Then we will be encouragingly and helpfully ushered out by those that torment us. Then our journey of freedom begins. Four hundred and thirty years and ten plagues later, it is finally our time to go.

We are being released from our captivity, our oppression, our humility. Our time to sit under the Passover blood that marked our door frames was short and sacred. This time of Passover will forever remind us of God's protection, of God's amazing peace for His people, of God's faithful fulfilling of promises, of God's redeeming and restoring our value and dignity by the blood on our doorposts. The experience is overwhelming and surreal. We cannot fathom, grasp, or contemplate what God has planned for us now. We just walk in faith and awe as we follow Moses, led by the LORD, out of Egypt.

It has been many hours since we started our journey, and no one has yet said a word. We are finally about to settle for a while so the animals can graze. Oh wait, I hear Moses now. He is telling us that this is a day to remember forever, and that every year we are to celebrate a great feast on the anniversary of our Exodus and to explain to our children what we are doing (Exodus 13:3-16). We all chuckle and laugh thinking how funny that is to think that we might forget. I must go for now, Moses is still telling us what else God wants us to do.

This, dear friend, is our story. This is the story of our ancestors, God's people, sitting under the Passover blood for a short but sacred time while being spared the sacrifice of their first born sons, unlike the Egyptians. The Israelites were sequestered in a place of quiet, contentment, peace and tranquility while the world around them was filled with terror, grief, crying, death and pain.

This is us safely secured behind the door frame stained with the blood of Jesus. As Ray Stedman describes it, "The angel of death passes over us. The angel of judgment will never pass our way because we are resting under the blood of the Lamb of God, a wonderful truth."[1]

The Passover story becomes our story, our heritage, our legacy the moment we believe, the defining moment when, "We have been made right in God's sight by faith, we have peace with God, because of what Jesus Christ our Lord has done for us" (Romans 5:1 NLT).

In the defining moment of our justification we are made right with God because we have come to accept the gift given to us in Jesus. At this defining moment at the foot of the cross, before God, He blesses us with an indescribable sense of tranquility and peace. It's a sacred time in our life when all the scrambling, the attempt at control, the confusion over a lack of meaning in our lives, a lack of direction or misdirection, the constant heaviness of a cold and lonely world, and the struggling of our individual life...ceases.

It's like we were ourselves homeless, meandering, sojourning, feeling lost as if we didn't fit in this world, feeling exhausted from having walked a long journey to arrive nowhere. As we approached what we thought the end of our destination, we were now inch by inch crawling along a sandy dry desert earth, only to realize our destination was merely a mirage.

Then suddenly we look up and see that we have somehow arrived at the doorstep of home, marked by blood stained sides and top. It even smells familiar at the doorstep with that roast lamb dinner cooking, and boy does it feel safe inside.

In those moments following the embarking action engaging us into a sacred covenant relationship with God, we enter the house where the Passover meal is about to be served, and we are

---

[1] http://www.blueletterbible.org/commentaries/comm_view.cfm?AuthorID=9&contentID=28&commInfo=2&topic=Exodus

astounded at the peace and tranquility of our wonderful Savior found within. I often think of the word *savor* when I think of our Savior. May we taste the amazing sweetness, or *savor* the flavor of a meal like we have never tasted before, like the Passover meal.

Then, just as the Israelites were soon asked to leave their place of sequestered peace to go into the world on a journey and follow the LORD, we too are asked to go into the world and follow the LORD. Within the life altering Christian experience captured in the fleeting Passover moments of our modern faith walk, our Christian experience is much like those of our forefathers. It's easy to think that the memory of such a unique and profound event filled with such peace and grace would stay with us forever, but somehow we come to forget. Just as our ancestors would forget, we too forget. Just as I forgot those beginning moments of peace through the saving grace of Jesus in that childhood kitchen in Indianapolis, Indiana.

God knew our sinful nature would eclipse the spectacular sunshine of our defining Passover moments. That is why the first thing His people are told to do upon exiting is to remember. Let us heed the instructions from our God to remember and proclaim to our children the story of our Exodus from captivity.

For in our modern faith walk, may every thought, word and deed be offered up to the LORD as a sacrifice readily and verbally proclaimed to our children, "I do this because of what the LORD did for me when we came out of Egypt" (Exodus 13:8). We too must work at remembering our heritage. We too must realize that we are leaving an old way of life behind for a new life of freedom. We too must tell the story to our children.

KEY MEMORY VERSES

1. On that day tell your son, 'I do this because of what the LORD did for me when I came out of Egypt. – Exodus 13:8
2. We have been made right in God's sight by faith, we have peace with God, because of what Jesus Christ our Lord has done for us. – Romans 5:1 NLT

QUESTIONS FOR DISCUSSION

1. Discuss the relevance of the Passover experience for us today. Is it any different than that of our ancestors?
2. Do you remember first believing? Share your experience or journal it.
3. What is it that God brings back to you through this Passover story that you may have forgotten?
4. What if we would do something every day to remember the story God has given us to claim as our defining moment instead of forgetting? What if we did that? What is it that you feel led to do in order to daily remember the grace and peace of your defining salvation moment?

4

DEFINING MOMENTS: THE CHRISTIAN EXPERIENCE REVEALED IN THE CROSSING OF THE RED SEA STORY

THE STORY CONTINUES

I last left you when Moses was talking to us about our first annual exodus festival. We had a big discussion about our firstborn sons. Moses was telling us that we owed God the lives of our firstborn sons. We wholeheartedly agreed that our first born sons now belong to the LORD. So we were to offer our firstborn males to the LORD, only the strange thing about it is that God allowed us to redeem our first born sons with the blood of an animal sacrifice instead (Exodus 13:12-13).

Who is this God that values the life of our children; that would spare us the sacrifice of them? We were overwhelmed with thankfulness and joy. Tears were running down our faces as we all hugged our children, and looked into their beautiful faces. Some are too young to understand the mercy God has shown us, but we will remember to tell them with each passing year of the exodus festival as they grow older.

We couldn't help but talk about God; our God that we follow must be full of love for His people. We have known no other God with such love. We don't really understand why the LORD would not keep our first born males for himself, but there is much about this wonderful God that we don't understand.

As our animals graze, we grieve for the Egyptians that lost their firstborn sons and firstborn male animals, if only they would have seen the power of this loving God in the first nine plagues. We wish they could have come to know our God. Maybe someday they will. We pray for them.

As for our journey, we are pressing on. We expected to travel through the Philistine territory, especially with so many of us and our livestock; it is the shortest route. But instead we are traveling a long route through the wilderness. We joke that if it were Moses leading us, we could see why we would be going through the wilderness, since he wandered in the wilderness for forty years before coming back to help us. But rest assured, it is the LORD leading us. The route we are taking is another one of those things we don't understand from our God.

I suppose you are wondering how we know it is the LORD leading us. It is a glorious, wondrous sight to see! You see, we have a pillar of cloud leading us during the day and a pillar of fire by night. One or the other is there all the time. It's amazing to think that we can travel any time of day or night since we can see all the time.

I must admit that it seemed kind of eerie at first when I realized this cloud was actually leading us. It just kind of hung there, always the same distance in front of us, and some around our sides like shepherd dogs keep a flock in line or heading in a direction. I feel so alive and have so much energy that I sometimes find myself wanting to run ahead just to see if I could actually pass through the clouds. But I don't.

We are about to set up camp for a while between the edge of the wilderness and the sea. The livestock need water and the

The Crossing of the Red Sea Story

children are really hungry. I must rest now. I'll journal more for you in a while.

We wake with a fright. Someone is waking us all up and yelling that they can see the Egyptians coming from far away. From the distant dust line we can see that there is a huge mass of them coming. The dust line seems miles long. Little do we know that the Pharaoh engaged all the forces in his army—all his horses, chariots and charioteers. We are shocked they have come for us. We did not anticipate this after everything we have gone through with them to be released. I mean they gave us anything we asked for in our travels, and hurried us along to leave. They wanted us to leave.

We are deathly afraid. We are in the worst place we could be for this to happen, being stuck between the wilderness and the sea. We are reviewing our options. They are coming at us from the wilderness side, so we can't go west. To the east is the Red Sea, and we don't have boats to take us across the water, it's certainly not shallow enough for the livestock or us to pass on foot, and it's too far to swim.

At this point, complete pandemonium has broken out. Women are crying and children are scared and huddled against their mother's bosoms seeking a comfort that seems completely elusive. The men are angry and are yelling at the LORD and Moses, more and more joining in the yelling as the seconds pass. I can hear some of the things my fellow Israelites are yelling, "Why did you bring us out here to die in the wilderness? Weren't there enough graves for us in Egypt? Why did you make us leave? Didn't we tell you to leave us alone while we were still in Egypt? Our Egyptian slavery was far better than dying out here in the wilderness!" (Exodus 14:11-12 NLT).

We all feel desperate, like we have already lost the battle. We knew we should have stayed in Egypt. It would have been better than dying out here in a bloody massacre of our people.

Pharaoh and his army are fast approaching and very near now. What I can't figure out is how Moses can be so calm. He is just standing there, looking towards the water's edge with everyone at his back yelling at the LORD and him. Are he and God indifferent to what is happening to us? It's almost like he is in a trance and can't even hear the cries of the people.

Wait, he is turning towards us. You should see the look on his face. It's a look of resolve and triumph and strength like we have never seen in a man. It silences our cries as we hold our breath. Within that held breath is a longing of hope and great anguish in anticipation of some word from God. Moses speaks in a loud voice with intonations of authority that yield encouragement without belittling us for our mass hysteria. "Don't be afraid. Just stand where you are and watch the LORD rescue you. The LORD himself will fight for you. You don't have to lift a finger in your defense"(Exodus 14:13-14 NLT).

Moses stops speaking, but we all hear a voice saying, "Get Moving" which makes no sense, move where? But it doesn't seem to matter as our mysterious cloud now completely surrounds us. We can't even see the Egyptians to our west. Moses is raising his shepherds' staff over the water. Our eyes watch in complete bewilderment as the wind blows from the west to the east. It's surreal. It's calming. This can't be… the water is parting and there is dry land, like a bridge appearing for us to walk on. Every woman, child, man and animal moves in unison within this cloud. We again are being shepherded by this wondrous cloud right through the parted waters with walls of water on each side, on the dry ground of the bottom of the sea!

We have been walking a long while now, and night has come. The pillar of cloud surrounding us has turned into a pillar of fire to light our way at night. Yet unbeknownst to us, when the cloud turned into a pillar of fire for us at night, the Egyptians following us have only darkness so they cannot find us.

The Crossing of the Red Sea Story

Many are now on the other shore of the Red Sea. I'm towards the back of the group where there is still complete silence since Moses turned to speak to us. The others that have completed the journey to the other side are a relieved group. I can see the smiles on their faces, and they look relaxed. Many are talking amongst themselves. I cannot see Moses in the crowd right now.

As I walk through these parted waters, there is a light spray of water on me from the walls of water. It's so cleansing. Since no one has spoken since we started the journey across the Red Sea, I'm not sure anyone else has thought about the Egyptians in a while. With the pillar of fire separating us and the Egyptians, we don't know where they are or how close they are. I can only assume they are still following us to the other side.

As the last of us arrive at the shore, it is early morning now. Every last one of us has passed through the Red Sea. We know the Egyptians are close because we can now hear that they are currently in a state of confusion and their chariot wheels are coming off. We hear them yelling, "Let's get out of here! The LORD is fighting for Israel against us!" (Exodus 14:25 NLT). And with that, Moses raised his hand over the sea again and the water walls come crashing down and roll into their usual place sweeping up the entire army of Pharaoh into the sea.

Only minutes have passed since we have seen the mighty power of God in the collapse of the water walls, and bodies are already washing up on shore. We know that not a single person will survive. We are struck with grief at the death of our tormentors, yet relieved that we have left our old life behind and will never have to go back.

We have yet to awaken from what seems like a dream to find ourselves alive, and with the realization that God fulfilled His promise by redeeming us with mighty power and the great act of judgment against our oppressors (Exodus 6:7b).

As it is finished today, all unbelievers now know that the God of the Israelites is the LORD. They also will come to know that

His chosen people have emerged on the other side, not just as a bunch Israelites that were once slaves and are now free, but as a glorified nation of people that move in unison following a mighty God. A God that leads His people, protects His people, and lights a path for His people. A God that delivers His people, redeems His people and restores His people's dignity.

They will come to know that His chosen nation, Israel, is not just freed of the hate for their past, their pain, their fatigue, their economic exploitation, and their humility. God's chosen nation of Israel is now free to embrace this grief for a lost people, their own oppressors.

Today, this is the freedom we are to embrace, this legacy of grief for a lost people. We have been given the power of forgiveness and redemption. And, in our healing, we now take up the fight, along with God, as His unified people.

Today, every Christian that has accepted the blood of Jesus can either continue to sit under the Passover blood or choose to walk through the waters of the Red Sea, leaving behind the old life and its ways to become a part of the unified people of God. At some point in our Christian experience we will hear God telling us to "get moving," and leave the past behind by going through the waters of the Red Sea to arrive on the other side with the unified Body of Christ.

Some might be half way through and some just stepped off the shoreline to walk on the bottom of the dry seabed. Others have arrived on the other side, and some are stuck between the wilderness and the Red Sea. This is our defining moment. To fully experience the Christian life as God intended, like our ancestors, we too must choose to follow our LORD across the Red Sea. When we do, we will leave self behind to arrive on the other side of the Red Seas as a member of the unified people of God.

In the time that we live until Jesus comes again, those that have passed through the Red Sea and are now on the shore have a choice to make. There is a second judgment coming on the nonbelievers of today, like the Egyptians of the past that were trapped in the Red Sea and received the fate of their judgment.

What is the choice? We can either work the shores as a glorified nation moving in unison and become the hand of hope that reaches out and saves as many as we can, as fast as we can, in any ways that we can until they are all saved, or what? What is the alternative? Is there an alternative?

Would we linger on the shores, pull a few out of the crashing waters, but once tired, take a break. During our break, we'll nourish our bodies with a meal, take a sleep and intend to go back the next morning to help.

But then the enemy comes. He lies. He shields us from hearing the cries of those drowning. What noise is in the way of us hearing the cries of the drowning? Schedules, business, piety, busyness, hesitation, fatigue, self-centeredness, school, children, watching TV, working out, sports, shopping, cleaning, walking the dog, laundry, reading, going to the doctor, surfing the web, going on a date, cooking, brushing our teeth, and back to eat to nourish the body and a sleep. It's so easy to not go back to the shore, isn't it?

These are our common, foundational defining moments that carry great relevance in our modern faith walk! We are fulfilling God's design in our Christian walk to leave self and the pain of the past behind and arrive on the other side as redeemed unified people. When we, by our faith, move beyond the comfort of our homes and churches and into the world, lead by a mighty and gracious God, miraculous things happen! Now we can work on building up from this foundation and reclaim other defining moments and promises!

KEY MEMORY VERSE

1. Don't be afraid. Just stand where you are and watch the LORD rescue you. The LORD himself will fight for you. You don't have to lift a finger in your defense. – Exodus 14:13-14

QUESTIONS FOR DISCUSSION

1. Can you relate to the things the Israelites said when they were facing their approaching captors again while stuck between the Red Sea and the wilderness?

2. What have you asked God about starting with "WHY"? Fill in the blank: God, why _____. Why did this happen to me or my family? Why do you allow…? Why does the World…? Why are we….?

3. Can you fill in this sentence? God, things were going along fine until you asked me to _____. I was far better off before _____.

4. Where are you in the journey? Are you still trapped under the oppression of slavery to the world and sin? Or have you left the land of your captivity? Are you camped between the wilderness and the sea? Or, have you begun to walk the bridge built for you, and move towards the other shore? Are you on the other shore? Have you already arrived a member of the unified people of God?

5. In the time we live in which we prepare for Christ to come again, we have the opportunity to help others cross over the Red Sea to be with us, a unified people working for Christ. What is your choice, to work the shores as the hand of hope pulling as many as we can to shore before the water drowns them, or go about our way trapped in a life of selfish focus? Are you doing what you should be now, or do you need to do something better than you have been?

5

Reclaim The Promise: Stop Learning Faith; Start Doing Faith

The Passover and the Red Sea are relevant, vibrant pieces of our Christian heritage. Once we recognize, claim, and allow ourselves to be realigned, connected, and rooted within these foundational experiences we can then come to explore other Biblical truths that define our modern faith walk in new-old ways.

One of the new-old ways that was revealed to me while I was in the soup kitchen comes down to the process of sanctification. Let's try to move beyond this church term of sanctification and refer to it as the process of *transformation*. In our modern faith walk, we have taken on the responsibility of growing our faith through learning, instead of the design by God to allow our works to continue to *transform* and mold our faith.

In essence we have moved from *doing* faith to *learning faith*, and this has huge implications that have crippled our ability to grow as God has designed. The enemy has been working overtime in establishing the cultural view that knowledge is power. God's plan to transform us is, in fact, about us embracing our weaknesses. In our weakness, all that we accomplish for the kingdom is about God and His power, and not about us.

We allow God to show His mighty power and in-breaking into the world through our service as weak vessels, empowered by, through, and for a great and glorious God. It is proclaimed in

2 Corinthians 4:5-7 (NLT) that, "You see, we don't go around preaching about ourselves. We preach that Jesus Christ is Lord, and we ourselves are your servants for Jesus' sake. For God, who said, 'Let there be light in the darkness,' has made this light shine in our hearts so we could know the glory of God that is seen in the face of Jesus Christ. We now have this light shining in our hearts, but we ourselves are like fragile clay jars containing this great treasure. This makes it clear that our great power is from God, not from ourselves."

For some reason, within God's design, He has chosen for us to help Him accomplish His purposes here on earth. The other part of this design is that God has given us the choice to do so or not. We are talking about the wonder and beauty and grace demonstrated in the verse, "My grace is sufficient for you, my power is made perfect in weakness" (2 Corinthians 12:9). The word root for "made perfect" is the Greek word *teleioō* which reveals a very intricate relationship between God's powers and accomplishing His purposes through us. The implications of this are astounding!

For instance, if we choose not to allow God to accomplish His purposes in our weakness, we render God's power useless, wasted, untapped and unused. On the other hand, it is amazing that the bottom line is God needs us. Let me say it this way. God needs you. God needs me.

Blessedly we have the Bible as a testament to the use of man throughout all history to help God accomplish His works. God could have easily led His people out of Egypt Himself. God did not have to partner with Moses to lead His people out of Egypt and across the Red Sea, but chose to do so.

God has exampled that His people along *with* God, are to work together to accomplish His works of saving souls, restoring justice, and bringing about world reconciliation. What a great and glorious, grace-filled God we serve that He would create a being which He has chosen to help Him accomplish His works. This wondrous

Stop Learning Faith; Start Doing Faith

design creates a purpose and meaning in our lives worth more than our hearts can comprehend.

When we allow God to work through us we come to represent God in this world. We are to show the world our God, *the* God, to help them see the nature of God. Within this process of demonstrating the nature of God to others, God designed the process of being transformed so that we are mysteriously and continually being changed into a more holy being. This results in further setting us apart as unique and different than the world in which we live. As God transforms us, we come to take on the very fiber and nature of God as representatives of Him to others in the world. "You are to be holy to me because I, the LORD, am holy, and I have set you apart from the nations to be my own" (Leviticus 20:26).

Therefore, it is imperative that we evaluate this process of transformation. The reality is that we need to reclaim the promise that God allows us to be transformed. God has provided and designed this way to be transformed. We must step out in faith to trust this process and realize we can do nothing to affect the process.

The process of transformation is a lifelong part of our journey, but also a daily one. We must evaluate from moment to moment whether to embrace our weaknesses and to trust and allow God to work through us. Or we let the deceit of the enemy take hold and destroy the mysterious beauty of the process of our being changed into the likeness of Christ, giving purpose in life to be a vessel for God.

The deceit is complicated and twisted into our humanness, but God will reveal His truth so that we can reclaim our works for God and His glory. Within our holy and transformed lives we are Christianity to the world. If that isn't a defining moment of our faith, I don't know what is!

The fact that God needs us to accomplish His works does elicit a certain amount of human fear and trepidation as we wholly feel our inadequacies to serve for God as ambassadors in the world. It is because of this fear and these inadequacies used by the enemy that our perception of how we can become useful to God is altered. The enemy will employ subtleties so minute that over time he has us come to doubt this process of being transformed. Yet we don't even realize that the memories of the promises of God are fading, until there passes the final moment when we now believe that we can do something to become more holy. We may even feel conviction that we must employ any means we can to become more holy to help God accomplish His works.

The awe of having God need us to accomplish His works is overwhelming. It's easy for us to question that with all our faults, errors, sins, wrong turns, bad habits, lack of discipline and lack of holiness, we could possibly do God's work. So we think that to honor God, we must take control and try to improve so that we can become more worthy ambassadors for God in the world. We set out to become more like God. With a mindset to work out all the kinks, the weaknesses, and the bad habits, we believe we can be of better use to God.

Have no doubt that when we are more holy that we more wholly serve God. It's just that we have been deceived into thinking that becoming more holy is defined by us, what we do and how we do it.

So, how do we take over this process of change? Why or how have we come to this point of thinking that we control or can contribute to this process of being more Christ-like? Are we doing it the way God designed for us to do it?

Here is where the problem starts. The most common problem that I have heard Christians speak is a reluctance to verbally testify about Jesus because of a fear of lack knowledge about God. What if someone asked a question about the Bible or God and we didn't know the answer?

We come to believe that we would be doing more damage than good by witnessing without knowledge. We live in a society where knowledge is power. So many of us go to those we may perceive as the local experts on God to get some knowledge. We go to church. We go to experience the worship of God at services, to hear sermons to figure out how to apply these scriptures to our daily life, and perhaps even go to Bible studies in our quest for an understanding of God.

Why must we know? The bottom line is that we believe to work for God, we need information. We live in the information age. We need answers. In our quest for answers, we have come to change the purpose of church from serving God to serving our relentless pursuit of knowledge. This pursuit of knowledge is what has formalized our Christianity.

It only makes sense that we would prepare ourselves for the experience of our faith walk. I mean, we wouldn't walk into a conference room to give a lecture on our job without knowledge of the matter. Where or what in our culture is success without knowledge or expertise?

Oh, but the way of the world is not God's way, is it? We know this, but the deceit is so great in this arena. We have to turn away from our desire to know *about* God and turn to knowing God, the God of relationships.

I fear that too often we are brought into the education/disciple-making process at church with a risk that the church experience becomes an ends to a mean, knowledge of God for personal selfish reasons. The true reality is that church should be a means to an end, experiencing and sharing God to the world.

When was the last time a person graduated from all the studies and experiences at church and was handed a diploma and sent out the door and told to go now and do what you were trained to do? We never feel like we have arrived. We just seek more knowledge under the selfish delusion that we are preparing for works that we may never come to do. We want to equip ourselves with knowledge and theology and an almost scientific approach to faith so that we will have the answers.

Tell me that knowledge isn't power in our world. In our humanness, it is almost impossible for us to grasp God's concept that His power is demonstrated through our weaknesses when our culture pounds the concept of "knowledge is power" into everything we do.

Our intentions seem honorable. We want to understand the word, the theology, and to be able to answer any question about Christianity and this God we follow. But just because the world may want answers in a box, doesn't mean we have to sit in our churches and wait for them to come to get answers from within the box of our churches where our local experts reside.

We point to the pastors and leaders of our church when someone walks in the door that wants to know about Jesus. We tell them to go to this service or that service, or this Bible study or that study. We have come to rely on them to be the experts, and have come to believe that we don't have the expertise to go into the world and proclaim the Good News as God designed. The fact of the matter is that Christianity is about having heart knowledge of God, not book knowledge. That is the soup kitchen way of living, loving, and honoring God.

If I could have an airplane flying around our country with one banner scripture on it, it would be, "Do not worry about what to say or how to say it. At that time you will be given what to say, for it will not be you speaking, but the Spirit of your Father speaking through you" (Matthew 10:19b-20). God doesn't need us to be transformed through knowledge of God, but through knowing God. That is how we are changed.

By focusing on our quest for knowledge of God, we have rendered ourselves useless to God. Knowledge is not power, weakness is. The formalization of our faith in the institutional church weakens the very muscle fiber of our legs that is needed to "Therefore, go and make disciples" (Matthew 28:19a). When we use the institutional church as a crutch, we exercise less of the muscles in our legs leading to atrophy creating legs that are useless, even totally paralyzed.

I'm pretty sure most Christians have heard of the great commission that we are to go and make disciples, but are we really doing this part of our work for God? Are you? Can you do it better? I think that God saw the potential problems in our humanness and our crutch to seek knowledge first before we felt we could go and make disciples.

I don't think it's a coincidence that the sentence Jesus speaks just before He tells us, "therefore go..." that He says to us, "All authority has been given to me in heaven and on earth. So, therefore go and make disciples" (Matthew 28:18-19). Jesus is saying like, "Hey ya'll (He could speak southern), don't forget that when you go out into the world and work for me, you do it through me, in my name, in my authority, in my power, in my knowledge, in my wisdom, in my spirit, ah... not yours."

Somewhere along the way we have mistakenly come to think that the process of being transformed is about us being empowered through knowledge to affect the process of becoming more Christ-like so that we think we will be better prepared for our work for Him. We come to seek knowledge of God instead of knowing God in order to feel empowered to become better ambassadors for Him. Here the twist of deceit happens when the purpose behind transformation becomes about knowing about God, rather than knowing God.

The authentic goal of becoming more holy or more Christ-like is to simply know God and the glory of God's grace and love through relationship, not knowledge. Real holiness comes from knowing God, not knowing the why and why not's of our beliefs, doctrines and faith issues.

It's about knowing God in our gut, the Greek root of *ginōskō* or the Hebrew root of *yada*. It's the type of knowing that is in your being, in your heart, in your bones. It's kind of like knowing how to write our name, or read a book, or ride a bike. In reading, we may not be able to explain the theory behind cognitive science in the areas of linguistics involving perception and action, brain imaging, and neurobiological methods of direct brain stimulation,[1] but we can read nonetheless. We don't need to know the theories behind reading to do it.

We need to get back to the roots of our informal Christianity. Becoming more knowledgeable about faith and God does not make us more holy or Christ-like, and does not lend us to becoming more useful to God to accomplish His works. In fact, we cannot do anything to become more sanctified, more holy. God himself transforms us. He set us apart (as symbolized in that we are to set the Sabbath apart) when He first refers to a new name for Himself in Exodus 31:13, "It helps you to remember that I am the LORD, who makes you holy (Yahweh Meqqadeshkem)."

As believers, the Holy Spirit is the one that continues to transform us to our Christ-likeness, not by anything we can do on our own. There is no amount of pew time, corporate worship, or Bible study that we can do that will give us a Bachelor, Master's or PhD in sanctification or preparation to go and change the world, although they do have their value in helping to further mold disciples.

Once we stop this obsession with knowledge to equip us for the works of God can we focus on reaching people for Christ with nothing but the hope of Jesus. We must stop learning faith and start doing faith!

It shouldn't matter whether we are a Day One Christian or a Day 30,000 Christian, the message is in our hearts and ready to be spoken from the moment we believe, repent and accept Jesus into our hearts. The truth of this is spoken in the scriptures, "That ye henceforth walk not as other Gentiles walk, in the vanity of their mind, having the understanding darkened, being alienated from the life of God through the ignorance that is in them, because of the blindness of their heart"(Ephesians 4:17b-18 KJV).

---

1   http://en.wikipedia.org/wiki/Cognitive_science#Language_processing

Knowledge acquired in our minds is merely for vain purposes to feel equipped to proclaim the Good News.

This quest for knowledge alienates us from God as we begin to count on our formal knowledge of God instead of our heart knowledge of God. Truly I tell you, all we need is the Holy Spirit that imparts knowledge in our hearts through hope to proclaim the Good News!

We cannot do anything to equip ourselves for our works for God. The apostle Paul addresses the very heart of this issue in his first letter to the Corinthians. He very carefully and succinctly contrasts non-believer ways with a believer's way in the matter of being equipped for works. He clarifies for us in saying, "Now about spiritual gifts, brothers, I do not want you to be ignorant. You know that when you were pagans, somehow or other you were influenced and led astray to mute idols" (1 Corinthians 12:1-2).

I believe the influence and mute idol he is referring to is they themselves. It's quite simple really. As a non-believer we would count on our own abilities, our learned skills and knowledge acquired through the process of education and experience. Paul is saying this is clearly not the way of believers, and not the way of spiritual gifts. This is the way of the world to be put aside.

He further contrasts the pagan ways with the skills for God's work described as, "There are different kinds of gifts, but the same Spirit. There are different kinds of service, but the same Lord. There are different kinds of working, but the same God works all of them in all men. Now to each one the manifestation of the Spirit is given for the common good" (1 Corinthians 12:4-7).

Paul describes how the Holy Spirit is the one that manifests itself in us to equip us with the gifts, service, and works to be done for the Lord for the common good of the Kingdom of God.

Before I served in the soup kitchen for the first time, I had much anguish. I was focused on my strengths and weakness and how they would affect my presence in this kitchen for Christ. My intentions seemed to be for the right reasons but I had concerns. I was concerned about how I would represent God to them.

How would they perceive me and my presence for Jesus? I contemplated what I would say to someone. What if I said something that they thought belittled them or showed how much I misunderstood them? How could I relate to them? What if I didn't know what to say in response to something they said? What if I said something that made them feel worse about themselves? What if they knew how uncomfortable I was being there?

It seems so clear and simple now, but I was fearful because I was counting on me and not the Holy Spirit. I hadn't yet learned to take a leap of faith and start doing faith. I wanted to run back into the church and prepare better. I was positive that I wasn't a mature enough Christian for this. I wasn't ready. The mute idol Paul was referring to was me, and I wanted to stay mute and not say anything out of fear of saying something wrong.

I had to get out of the way, and let God take over. This wasn't about me and what I had to offer or not. This was about walking into a place and counting on God to manifest himself in me, a messed up self-centered immature Christian. As I walked into that kitchen God took a large pair of lopping shears and chopped off a few dead branches. Pruning was on its way, real growth was bound to happen. That is the soup kitchen way.

The soup kitchen way is the way of approaching our work for God as originally intended. It's about the radically new-old way of doing faith, not learning faith to therefore go into the world and make disciples. The scriptures abound with examples of how our faith is to be lived out as disciples of Christ. Let me reiterate the point of doing faith by reviewing the stories of the first disciples that encountered Christ.

The first documented action we have by one of the original disciples is Andrew who goes and tells his brother about Jesus (John 1:41). The next example in the story God provides us is about Philip who immediately takes off to tell others who he has found (John 1:43-45). Jesus could have stopped them, but didn't.

Jesus didn't yank them back by their tunics and say, "Wait! You need to know more before you go telling people about me."

There is no egg incubation period where Jesus takes them in and requires them to learn things in order to go and proclaim the Good News. Jesus allows them to go immediately with only the joy and hope of salvation on their lips. All we need to engage in works for God is in our moment at the cross when we accept the gift of salvation. It's the joy of our salvation moment like the first disciples that bursts forth from our heart of hearts like Christmas morning joy as a child. Let's visit this moment in history.

I am six years old, and in bed on Christmas Eve. We set out the cookies and milk by the twinkling lights of the Christmas tree. Santa is coming soon, but I can't fall asleep. I'm too excited about him coming. Finally sleeping, Santa came and spread good cheer with stockings full of goodies, and a few treasured presents wrapped under the tree. I awake around 4:30 A.M. and instantly remember its Christmas morning! I run down stairs to see if Santa has come. Wow! He has! The stockings are full (as our hearts are full.) The presents beautiful (like the gift of salvation), the cookie is eaten (as we have partaken of His body in remembrance). The milk is gone too (as we partake of the blood of Christ).

Then, bursting forth with unrestrained joy (like the joy of our salvation), I yell, "Santa was here! Wake up, wake up!" My little feet hurriedly carry me back upstairs to mom's room. I pounce on the bed, and yell some more, "Did you hear me? Santa was here! He filled our stockings! He left all kinds of presents under the tree! He ate the cookie and drank the milk! Let's go! Let's go!" And you know the rest of the story.

Oh the joy of Christmas morning! Even though in my real life experience, my sister woke up first every year and solely proclaimed the good news and joy of Christmas morning in our household, God gives each of us a voice and chance to proclaim the Good News of the joy of salvation every day or any day we choose!

Christmas joy is the simple joy that our salvation brings us with hearts full of God's grace and love from the gift of salvation found in the body and blood of Jesus! Like a child on Christmas morning, we want to go around shouting about the saving grace of Jesus.

Let's fight to keep a hold of the joy of our salvation experience to want to share it with anyone we can, in any ways we can instead of running back into the building of the church and asking, "So, what it is I need to know about God before I go?"

We already know it – the hope of Jesus. That is all we need to start doing faith. That is all we need to go and make disciples. That is all we need to engage in the works of our God in this world. It is then, when we go into the world of the broken, the hurting, and the lost, that we really begin to know and experience God as we were designed. May we come to be Christians who are doing faith, and not just learning faith. It all works together in a miraculous way as we reclaim promises that go hand in hand with our transforming moments as Christians.

KEY MEMORY VERSES

1. Do not worry about what to say or how to say it. At that time you will be given what to say, for it will not be you speaking, but the Spirit of your Father speaking through you. – Matthew 10:19b-20

2. All authority has been given to me in heaven and on earth. So, therefore go and make disciples. – Matthew 28:18-19

3. It helps you to remember that I am the LORD, who makes you holy (Yahweh Meqqadeshkem). – Exodus 31:13

4. That ye henceforth walk not as other Gentiles walk, in the vanity of their mind, having the understanding darkened, being alienated from the life of God through the ignorance that is in them, because of the blindness of their heart – Ephesians 4:17-18 KJV

Questions for Discussion

1. Are you learning faith or doing faith?
2. What if we realized that every time we say no to God because we are afraid or too busy with the things of this world that we render His mighty power useless?
3. What if it wasn't about our fear of being uncomfortable around the needy, and it was about their fear of being alone, and hungry and lacking dignity?
4. What if we all let go of the quest for knowledge for the purposes of effective evangelism and truly trusted the Holy Spirit to provide the ways and the words?
5. Discuss the joy of your Christmas mornings and the excitement and joy of the moments. Can you hold to the related feelings of relief and joy in your moment at the cross? Do you remember those moments?
6. Have you ever felt "prepared" to go and make disciples for the kingdom? Why or when?
7. Do you believe you are prepared to bring the good news to others?
8. Is there room to let go of your control of your sanctification process? Are you willing to trust God's design for being transformed?
9. Do you now believe that the hope of Jesus is all you need to go and make disciples?

6

RECLAIM THE PROMISE: GOD'S DESIGN TO KNOW HIM

"To Know Him Is to Love Him" is a song written by Phil Spector, inspired by words on his father's tombstone. It was first recorded by his first vocal group, the only one of which he was a member, the Teddy Bears. The words to this song came to my mind when I was trying to decide which topic should be placed where in the flow of the book. I couldn't decide if you should first read the chapter about the love factor followed by the knowing God chapter, or the chapter about knowing God followed by the love chapter.

As I prayed about this, pondered it, wondered about it, wrestled with it, I was awakened the next morning with this saying on my mind "To Know Him Is to Love Him." I didn't know if it was a poem, a song, or some famous quote. All I knew was it was stuck in my head. I kept hearing it in my mind over and over again.

Then I realized, after a few cups of coffee, that this was the answer to my question. It made complete sense in the way of things that you must know something before you can love something, so the chapters should follow the natural order of things. As always, God faithfully provided the answer. So we will first talk about reclaiming the promise of God's design to know him, followed by the love chapter.

There are many doors from which to enter into the house of the Christian life, but I will start with the front door, the door behind which Jesus is standing with open arms. He ushers us in with an arm linked in ours to take us for a walk and a talk. He tells us so many wonderful things.

When we get to the heart of the matter, God created us for fellowship. God wants to build a relationship with each and every one of us. God's idea of a relationship is coming to know and understand each other, and the key to understanding God is to understand Jesus. Jesus tells us that "I am the way and the truth and the life. No one comes to the Father except through me" (John 14:6). "You do not know me or my Father," Jesus replied. "If you knew me, you would know my Father also" (John 8:20).

We need to reclaim this promise that Jesus is the way, the truth and the life. This is more than Jesus being our Savior; this is Jesus being our friend, our hope, our focus, our heart. It is reclaiming the promise to know God by knowing Jesus. I mean really knowing Him and His nature, His heart, His soul, His love, His humbleness, His compassion, His grief for the least of these. Who wouldn't want to know more of Him this way?

All I'm asking of you is to wonder, is there room for you to know Him better and deeper? You may have studied at length about Jesus and His life and ministry, but until you meet Him face to face you won't really know Him. But the good news of this promise is that we don't have to wait until death or the second coming to meet Him face to face. That is the beauty of this promise that we will take a look at.

Think of it this way, you can learn about Nelson Mandela, read biographies, even autobiographies, watch movies about his life, hear people talk about him that have met him, and come to know about Nelson Mandela. But, until you meet the man himself you are missing crucial components about really knowing Nelson Mandela. What about his tone of voice or hand gesture when he reaches out to cup a child's face in his hands, or the soulful look in his eyes when preaching with passion about ending apartheid?

There is knowing about Nelson Mandela, and there is experiencing Nelson Mandela. There is knowing about Jesus, and there is experiencing Jesus. Have we forgotten that we love a God who is alive and is available and accessible to each and every one of us?

So where or how do we meet Jesus face to face today? Yes, we can know about Jesus through the scriptures, through Bible studies, movies and books. But how can we experience Jesus in our midst, personally, right here, right now?

I'm so glad you asked. Let's take a look at the first time Jesus reveals who He is and what He is here for to the disciples. This gives us direction as to where our focus should be, where we can still find him today.

"The scroll of the prophet Isaiah was handed to him (Jesus). Unrolling it, he found the place where it is written: 'The Spirit of the Lord is on me, because he has anointed me to preach good news to the poor. He has sent me to proclaim freedom for the prisoners and recovery of sight for the blind, to release the oppressed, to proclaim the year of the Lord's favor.' Then he rolled up the scroll, gave it back to the attendant and sat down. The eyes of everyone in the synagogue were fastened on him, and he began by saying to them, 'Today this scripture is fulfilled in your hearing'" (Luke 4:17-21).

Folks, there is a 100% guarantee that we will know Jesus better by serving the least of these! That is the promise within this mysterious and wondrous design of how God allows us to personally experience him. The tragedy is that it has lost its relevance in our modern faith walk.

The first thing we must ponder in these verses is why He was to bring the Good News to the poor, as in the meek and the humble. This is not related to the fact that He is quoting scripture from the scroll of yore, and fulfilling the prophecy of Isaiah 61:1-2. This is looking at it from the beginning of the God's plan, even before it was prophesied by Isaiah. Why not some other group, who doesn't need the message of the Good News?

He could have chosen to bring it to the selfish, or those who are rich and idolize money, or those who are deceived by and hunger for power, or the pious Pharisees, the proud, etc. There was a moment when God had to decide to communicate this to us and the impact it would have, bound up in the choice of whose name would complete this sentence,

"The Spirit of the Lord is on me, because he has anointed me to preach the good news to the _____" (Luke 4:18).

So, why is it the poor? Why do they receive the grace and favor of being the focus of the salvation message of God? Because in them is He. Seriously, stop and contemplate the question. Why would God declare the message of salvation is for the poor? As I experienced in the soup kitchen, the answer God revealed to my heart was that as I came to know them, I came to know Jesus. Not only is He *in them*, He *is* them!

You know those holographic images where you move a picture image and it changes from one thing to another, back and forth? Well, that is what it is like with how we can experience Jesus in our midst today. It's like a holographic image where one second it's the face of the poor, the humbleness of the poor. Then, move the picture a little, and the next second it's the face of Jesus, the humbleness of Jesus!

Amazingly, wondrously, in them, through them, we meet Jesus personally. Through them we begin to understand this God that became a man who was himself homeless, hungry, hurting, thirsty and imprisoned. It is here that we encounter the very nature of God that cannot be learned in any other way.

Dear reader, let's not miss the mysterious and wondrous design of the way God allows for us to encounter him. For me it was in the soup kitchen. Being able to meet Jesus face to face in the least of these is truly a miracle and the heart of the blessing of the soup kitchen experience–wherever it is you are led to serve in this world. It will change and deepen your relationship in unexplainable ways

Reclaim the Promise: God's Design to Know Him

as you come to know the very heart of God. In that soup kitchen, where I met face to face with Jesus, I discovered a desire like no other, to have a heart like God's.

One of the greatest scripture treasures that directs us to this inexplicable way to encounter Jesus is when He talks about judgment day to His disciples. "'... for I was hungry and you gave Me food; I was thirsty and you gave Me drink; I was a stranger and you took Me in; I was naked and you clothed Me; I was sick and you visited Me; I was in prison and you came to Me.' "Then the righteous will answer Him, saying, 'Lord, when did we see You hungry and feed You, or thirsty and give You drink? When did we see You a stranger and take You in, or naked and clothe You? Or when did we see You sick, or in prison, and come to You?' And the King will answer and say to them, 'Assuredly, I say to you, inasmuch as you did it to one of the least of these my brethren, you did it to Me'" (Matthew 25:35-40 NKJV).

Oh, the grace in these lines of scripture! Jesus is very explicit in saying that when these things are done to the least of these that it is like doing it to Jesus himself, not *for* Him or *like* Him, but *to* Him. I also want to point out that the pronoun chosen in these scriptures for who is doing the deeds is "you." Jesus could have chosen any pronoun, like someone instead of you. But, it's not about "someone." He doesn't say, "Someone gave me food, someone gave me drink, someone took me in, someone clothed me, someone visited me." The use of the pronoun "someone" would be more elusive or random, or broader in scope. Instead, He spoke of these deeds being done by "you" which is consistent with Jesus' message that this is personal. It's about an intimate connection between two people, again resonating relationship. He makes it about you and Him. It's not someone, it's you, dear loved ones of Christ!

There are more treasures still in this verse. Brad Jersak describes this miraculous experiencing of Jesus in the least of these like this, "you see me in them when you remember that I literally became a peasant, a refugee, a prisoner. I live with the least, the lost, and the lowly; through them, you will meet me and come to know me, my heart, and my ways."[1] He further states that, "the least of these hold the keys to spiritual doors of God's kingdom that are inaccessible apart from their unlikely aid. To use Isaiah's imagery (57:14-15), the "lowly" remove boulders and obstacles that would otherwise block our ways to Mount Zion. We often imagine that by attending to the "least" (literally, "little ones"), we were doing them a favor. But when we discern the presence of Christ in them, and an undercover visitation of God, we realize the least are real mentors with spiritual keys."[2] Make no mistake about the value of learning about the nature of God by meeting Him face to face in service to the least of these.

Now dear reader, let's further evaluate the latter part of Isaiah's message that Jesus spoke in Luke 4 that He is also sent, "to bind up the brokenhearted, to proclaim liberty to the captives, and the opening of the prison to them that are bound" (Isaiah 61:1-2; see also Luke 4:14-21). What exactly does this mean in our faith experience today?

The mission, Jesus' mission, our mission, our Christian directives are clearly laid out before us as Jesus proclaims in Luke 4. We are to bring the Good News to the poor that their Savior has arrived, and to take on social justice issues, to right the wrongs of the world. This is where our work begins and ends. Why is this now our job, you ask? The truth is revealed in our salvation experience. Can we all agree that through the salvation experience we are afforded the transforming power of the Holy Spirit for the purpose of becoming more Christ-like? If we can, then we must come to agree why that is so. Why are we transformed? That is so we can represent Christ in the world, so that we can continue the work Jesus started long ago. We are kingdom agents. Our mission

---

[1] Leadership Magazine, Fall 2007, "On the Margins, Guides to The Kingdom," pg. 32.
[2] *ibid*

is laid out very clearly in 1 John 2:6, "Whoever claims to live in Him, must walk as Jesus did." It doesn't say we *might* walk. It says we *must* walk.

So how, where, and with whom did Jesus walk? Jesus so beautifully and clearly shows us the way. Jesus walked with, ate with, fished with, talked with, prayed with, mourned with the sick, the prostitute, the tax collectors and other outcasts and downtrodden. The heart of Jesus is to befriend them, to care for them, to love them, and restore their dignity by believing in them, listening to them, eating with them, and spending time with them. God designed it so that when we come to spend time with the needy, the least, the lost we come to see them and how they got there and want to help them move beyond what ails, oppresses or inhibits them from gaining dignity, life, purpose and hope!

Anything that is broken, Jesus came to fix. He came to bind up the brokenhearted by making them whole. Anything that is out of balance, He came to reconcile. It is further summed up in the scriptures as, "For God was pleased to have all his fullness dwell in him (Christ), and through him to reconcile to himself all things, whether things on earth or things in heaven, by making peace through his blood, shed on the cross" (Colossians 1:19-20).

What that means for us is to also work at restoring wholeness to not only those people that are broken like the hurting, the grieving, the sick, the lonely, the outcasts, and the down-trodden, but also what oppresses them. We are to free the captives which I'll call those held against their will by the forces of society that trap them in situations of oppression, poverty, slavery, homelessness, hunger, lack of immunizations, lack of clean water, and mental ailments without relief.

We, like Christ, are to open and unbind those that are in prison from bondage to sin, bound within the prison cell of self, behind the bars of self-centeredness, ensnaring a soul to feel no hope and see no light. Those are in the prison of a life with no meaning.

This second part of our mission is the essential part that I missed somewhere in my Christian learning experience, and I fear I am not the only one. Why didn't I know that I am also to work in the world to right the wrongs? And what does the least of these have to do with this? Why didn't I understand that in order for us to do these things we must come to understand the complexity of these situations? To be able to help change the systems, the policies, the power struggles, and the mind sets that foster these conditions and keep the least of these oppressed, imprisoned, and held captive, it is for us to care.

In an essence, that means we should be deeply involved in these causes in order to render solutions to righting the wrongs of the world as Jesus set out to do.

So how has it come to pass that we have lost this mission within our Christian imperatives to follow Jesus this way? It's like we separated our missions from each other. Our mission is stated to bring the Good News AND...etc., it doesn't say to bring the Good News OR...etc... This would be like a husband in a family unit that chose to be in the family, but only chose the role of husband instead of fulfilling the role of husband and father. It just wouldn't make sense, would it? It would almost seem impossible for a husband and father to be in a household and only function as one and not both. How could a father separate them?

How could we separate our mission laid before us? How could we set aside our role and function for the kingdom to work on social justice issues? How do the words of separation of church and state make you feel? Are we living in a culture that demands we back religion out of our policies and government? Has a secular government movement taken on the social justice issues so that the matter can be completely removed from the spiritual works of Christians? You bet.

There is another factor at play here as well. There is the issue of the missing list and the enemy using this weapon of ambiguity again. Why or how doesn't matter as much as to know that the

Reclaim the Promise: God's Design to Know Him 57

enemy is behind it. But it seems more natural for us to focus on the things we can easily grasp, like the things God tells us to do. We have a list of such as the Commandments, the fruit of the spirit, and several lists of spiritual gifts. Do you love lists as much as I do? Lists from God give us great accountability!

Somehow we have come to focus on the work within the church with our spiritual gifts, perhaps because there is a neat and tidy list to refer. But where is our list of social justice issues to work on? There isn't one. Perhaps we would see social justice issues as more relevant in our modern faith walk, as part of our daily mission for God if there were a list in the Bible like this:

- some have the gift of developing and distributing immunizations to eliminate 80% of child deaths from preventable diseases
- some have the gift of working with the homeless and should serve them to restore dignity
- some have the gift of redistributing food supplies so no child goes hungry in their community, ever.
- some have the gift of advocacy for the fair treatment of employees found in sweat shops
- some have the gift of vision to change the tax system for small business owners to alleviate the burden of 100% of social security and medicare tax when regular employees only pay half
- some have the gift of kindness towards orphans and widows, to go and love them
- some with the gift of political action, make sure the government system remains aligned with God's morals
- some with the gift to serve in prison ministry, do so with compassion and patience
- some have the gift to impact housing costs to reduce homelessness

- some with the gift of working with abused children, serve with love and joy
- some have the gift to bring clean water systems to third world countries that would alleviate most of the deaths by diseased water
- some have the gift to organize and distribute medical supplies to disadvantaged elderly
- some have the gift of organizing a regional walk to raise money for a cure for breast cancer

But there isn't such a list. This indirect pronouncement of our work for the kingdom of God seems to have lost its vision behind the ambiguity factor used by the enemy. So somewhere along the way we came to cling to the lists we have like the spiritual gifts lists. But, the scripture message remains that we all are responsible for taking on Christ-like missions to reconcile all things within our homes, our streets, our communities, our cities, our country and our world. If that isn't a radically new-old way of experiencing God, I don't know what is!

OK, I feel the need for a side bar conference, join me for a second...don't shut down on me and this message. It is the heart of the Soup Kitchen for the Soul message. It may be uncomfortable, you may have thrown up a wall, you may not agree with me, or you may not see the relevance for your Christian walk. But, please keep an open mind and an open heart to receive the rest of the message God has placed on my heart to share with you.

Once we put on the eyes of Jesus to walk about and look for those to serve as He did, we'll see them and the things that keep them imprisoned and in chains. As Henry David Thoreau said, "It's not what you look at that matters, it's what you see." The soup kitchen way of seeing is with the heart of God. With the heart of God dwelling in us, we become compelled to work in these ways for the kingdom of God, ambiguity abounding or not.

The ways and means of serving God in our mission to restore harmony and peace in this process of reconciliation are endless, but fear not! It could be about working towards understanding the plight of the hungry so you can engage in ways to alleviate it. One might ask if it is a resource problem, a distribution problem or perhaps a producing problem? A local problem might be having adequate funds to buy food due to high housing costs or low income levels, and yet across the world it is a production problem to produce vegetation with scarce water resources.

Some might come to see and nurture the lonely by visiting the sick so they will know they are not forgotten in their isolation in the ICU behind glass walls.

It's working to understand how people become homeless and advocating for their dignity and fair treatment without the bias of stereotyping.

It's plugging into a group that teaches immigrant parents English to better function in our society.

It's about mentoring a child in elementary school that will be held back because she can't even write her name. It's about wanting to find out why she can't and what you can do about it. Does she have a learning disability or is it something else? You won't know until you spend time with the child that will have you come to understand that her sole concern and focus is on whether her mom will be beaten again today by her daddy. It is then that you understand that learning to write her name doesn't seem important in the scope of her life. The frustrating thing may be that you probably cannot save her literally from her parents or the home life she has, but you can work towards saving her by praying for her, loving her and showing the grace of God and the very face of Jesus in you. We can also work to advocate the plight of the abused and work to stop the cycle of abuse through education and agencies in that arena.

The opportunities to be Jesus in this world are endless. We have much work to do to right the wrongs before Jesus comes again to restore the world! But we cannot and should not wait for Jesus to come to do this. It is our job while here on earth! We are Jesus' hands and feet. Jesus clearly passed us the torch in His prayer to the Father for the disciples, "As you sent me into the world, I am sending them into the world" (John 17:18). God designed us to move in the world for Jesus now. He chose to have us participate in understanding and healing what ails society to bring about direction, purpose and meaning in our lives. We are it. Last I knew while writing this, Jesus hasn't come back yet. There is no one to do the job at hand but us.

How can we not be compelled to work in these ways? Perhaps a feeling of being overwhelmed swells in your heart. Don't be! That is the work of the enemy. You don't need to do it all. You just have to find your niche.

The easy way to do that is to just try some things. You don't need to join a mission team in some foreign third world country, although you might want to some day. I love the saying, "Think globally, act locally."[1] You may not have some amazing 'a-ha moment' where you will just wake up and know where it is you are effective in fighting the good fight. It takes time and effort.

Take the time to start educating yourself on things in your community. Who are the non-profit groups in your community? What groups does your local church support already? Review general topics on the internet about hunger, child hunger, immigration issues, homelessness, infant mortality in third world countries, breast cancer, child labor camps, sweat shops, human trafficking, child pornography, domestic violence, mental illnesses, veteran's issues, etc.

Be patient with yourself in this process, but diligent. It may take months or years of awareness training to see where God leads you to move in. Just let me reassure you that not one second of time spent on training your eyes to see as God sees is ever wasted! Remember our defining moments of the Red Sea Experience, all

---

1   First attributed to Scots Planner in 1905

Reclaim the Promise: God's Design to Know Him

God commands you to do is to get moving. You don't need to know where you are going. Just trust that He will lead the way and guide you to where you are supposed to be just like your ancestors before you.

In so doing, everyday you will come to better know and understand the heart of Jesus, and if you know the heart of Jesus, you know God! Can I get another Amen?

When we carry His love and grace to the poor, the brokenhearted, the imprisoned, the lonely and the needy, they are fulfilling the purposes of being spiritual mentors for us. Through their contact with us, with the help of the Holy Spirit, they remove the boulders on the way to Mount Zion. All the while we are fulfilling the purposes of reconciling the rights of their wrongs from loving them, in which we come to understand their plight. This allows us to see ways to right the wrongs and then work towards changing and correcting them.

This beautiful and wondrous design of reciprocity is almost beyond comprehension. Thank goodness God gives us the ability to experience this in the soup kitchens of the world so we can feel it instead of just learning about it. Heart knowledge is much more important and useful than book knowledge.

It is time, dear friend, to reclaim God's promise that we can know His heart and His nature through those that He chose to reveal Himself in, the poor, the meek, the humble, the least of these.

Seek God's face in them. I imagine this is like asking you to put your hand on a hot stove burner. You have learned that it is painful, so you rationally wouldn't reach out and touch it. If you hadn't learned that yet, if you did touch a hot burner, your body would instinctively react to pain through removal of your hand. It would only take milliseconds for you to pull your hand back. Our brains are wired to have us avoid pain.

Remember the parable of the rich man and Lazarus in Luke 16? Lazarus was the beggar covered with sores that had dogs licking his wounds. The rich man saw and passed by him often at the gate of his home with no action, no acknowledgment, no remorse. Lazarus was too painful to look at, let alone talk to, to bring him into his home, or to provide food or comfort to help him.

We can all relate to something too painful to even look at, can't we? That is why the enemy is so effective in hindering us from wanting to go to our local Lazaruses of the world and help them. It hurts to help. That is the compelling nature of compassion and the heart of God. It aches.

Yes, your heart will ache. You will instinctively want to pull back to avoid feeling this pain of the world. Don't! Let go of the fear and the lies of the enemy to avoid them and the pain they represent. Instead embrace them, embrace the pain, the hurt and the sorrow, feel and know them as Jesus did. As you come to know them, you will come to know Jesus' heart and nature. And to know Him is to love Him, and them. It will be the experience of a lifetime! God promises!

Key Memory Verses

1. I am the way and the truth and the life. No one comes to the Father except through me. – John 14:6
2. "You do not know me or my Father," Jesus replied. "If you knew me, you would know my Father also." – John 8:20
3. The Spirit of the Lord is on me, because he has anointed me to preach good news to the poor. He has sent me to proclaim freedom for the prisoners and recovery of sight for the blind, to release the oppressed, to proclaim the year of the Lord's favor. – Isaiah 61:1-2a, Luke 4:18-19

4. For God was pleased to have all his fullness dwell in him (Christ), and through him to reconcile to himself all things, whether things on earth or things in heaven, by making peace through his blood, shed on the cross. – Colossians 1:19-20

5. As you sent me into the world, I am sending them into the world. – John 17:18

QUESTIONS FOR DISCUSSION

1. Is there room for you to know Jesus better and deeper? Are you willing to meet Him face to face to have the boulders removed on your way to Mount Zion?

2. What if I told you that there was a 100% guarantee that you would know Jesus better by serving the least of these?

3. What if even half the Christians in the world, or 1.3 billion of us committed to move into the world of the needy to meet Jesus face to face? What do you think the implications would be?

4. What if we delivered food to the hungry, and didn't just send it?

5. What if we delivered help to the imprisoned, and didn't just send it?

6. Discuss the ambiguity of our works to help the least of these. Do you see how the enemy uses this to keep us from engaging in ways to come to know Jesus' heart?

7. Do you understand and believe the design of God's mission for us laid out in Jesus' pronouncement of who He is and why He came? Do you understand and believe that is what we, too, are to do?

8. What if it was about having one hour a week set aside to serve the hungry, and it wasn't about one extra hour of watching television?

9. What if it was using your one hour a day surfing the web to surf websites and articles on homelessness causes and solutions, or childhood deaths from hunger related issues, or domestic abuse, or deinstitutionalization in relation to homelessness, or…?

7

DEFINING MOMENTS: WE ARE A PECULIAR PEOPLE DEFINED BY LOVE

Yes, to know Jesus is to love Jesus. One flows from the other. But what should also flow from knowing and loving Jesus is a love for others. It's how God designed us to be a peculiar people defined by love.

One of the greatest defining moments of our faith is in the love poured out for us as, "God so loved the world that he gave his one and only Son, that whoever believes in him shall not perish but have eternal life" (John 3:16). The love factor abounds in the sacred text of our Bible. The love bestowed upon us in the giving of God's son to us is key.

We must now move forward in our evaluation of the love factor under the assumption that it is a defining and unique characteristic of who we are because that is who God is. We are told in Romans 13:14, "Rather clothe yourselves with the Lord Jesus Christ, and do not think about how to gratify the desires of the sinful nature."

Within this scripture treasure, the Word reveals to us to do something, to take on the appearance of Christ. Let's think of this as God telling us that to move in this world we are required to put on our 'Jesus jackets' to identify us as a peculiar people defined by love. As we put on our 'Jesus jackets' we can envision aligning our spirit and heart with His spirit and heart by focusing on loving and serving others. It's like when a regular person walks into a hospital and puts on their doctor jacket. They are changed. People know they are a doctor by the jacket they wear.

In the same way, people should know that our actions rooted in love identify us as a peculiar people! We should so love, serve, and help that we stick out like a sore thumb. People should see what we do and feel compelled to ask, "What's up with her?" "Why does she do what she does?" Maybe one day they will ask us directly and we'll be able to respond, "...because I serve a mighty, loving, and gracious God! Let me tell you about Him." One such little town clothed in 'Jesus jackets' I passed through is a perfect example of a community that displays such peculiar ways.

My family and I were driving from Florida to Tennessee for a relaxing vacation. Our route had us driving through much of Georgia. We spent the night in northern Georgia, and continued on our road trip the next morning.

As we started out on the highway, we noticed our SUV had a certain shimmy to it that didn't feel right. My husband and I talked and both had felt it the night before, but it seemed worse this morning. Something was definitely wrong. So, we decided to pull over at the next logical exit with a station that had help for tires. I had seen a sign some ways back for a truck station and thought that might be a good place.

We found the place and the truck stop. This was no ordinary truck stop! It was an 18-wheeler fixer-upper place! They worked on the cabs, trailers, tires, and the works. When we walked into the warehouse space to find a person amongst these mighty trucks, I realized our SUV was probably too small to even fit up on one of their lifts.

We found a sweet man we'll call "George" who helped us. He told us our car was too small to be worked on there, but said he would take a look at our car anyway. So, my husband gave him the male version of what was wrong. Then I gave him the female version of what was wrong. All I could think of was that this guy was really nice or really smart.

You see, he even seemed to understand the female version of the description I was giving, or played along sweetly. If any man has ever heard a woman describe a car, plumbing or electrical problem, you know what I'm talking about. We speak a different language that probably makes no sense in the world of 'male' sense. If cars, plumbing, and electrical can be touchy-feely, we make it so. And, if any woman has ever had to describe what is wrong with her car, you know what I'm talking about. The men often have a blank look when you are telling them what you think is wrong with your car. Talking to the Truck Doctor George about my car problems was like being in therapy. The man made me feel so important. I was listened to with great respect. This encounter with Truck Doctor George was very unusual, or dare I say "peculiar!"

So, he took our car for a drive and came back to explain to us (not just my husband- he actually looked at me, too, as he explained) that he believed we had tire separation (sounds like a therapy session to me). So, Dr. George sent us off into this little town to a place that could help us with our tire problems.

Before we left, Dr. George called the place where he was sending us, and personally talked to the man that he told us to see. He explained what he thought was wrong, and told him to help us out. How sweet to go out of his way to call for us!

We arrived at the tire center to find our personal contact, arriving like a friend; we say "Dr. George sent us over." It was like coming home. They responded, "Oh yes, we've been expecting you." So, they checked our car in with an expected two hour delay.

We have a six-year-old and three-year-old on a road trip. Now it's time to entertain the little ones. We play Frisbee in a nearby parking lot. That lasted about four minutes with only 116 more minutes to go. Luckily, there is a train station about two blocks over. We walk over there, hang out, board a parked engine and play near some tracks. We have a throwing contest to see who can throw rocks and hit the metal rails and make a cool sound. Then we head back towards the tire center.

There are two restaurants across the street from the tire center. So, we decide to get some lunch at the restaurant that has a scripture on it as part of their sign. On our two block journey to the restaurant, a nice lady driving by asks if we need a ride. How sweet, but, "No thanks," we respond.

How peculiar was that in a world where we don't have time to do such things? How peculiar was that in a world where someone might conclude you're a kidnapper if you offer to pick up a stranger? How peculiar was that in a world where you certainly don't stop to ask to give strangers a ride since the strangers might be dangerous people? Seriously, I don't mean to belabor the point, but just a simple act of kindness to help a stranger like offering a ride is something unusual today. Fear often inhibits our kindnesses. You can definitely feel something different in this town. We're beginning to feel like we are in our very own "Truman" town like the movie, The Truman Show.

So, we arrive at the little restaurant. We order our drinks and food, and wait. And wait. And wait. We built buildings out of all the plastic butter containers. We reviewed our rock collection.

Now, we city folk can wait, don't get me wrong. I mean we had no place to go anyway. We aren't impatient, but the kids were getting restless. So, like all good parents, we send the kids off to the bathroom to play in the water and soap at the sinks. Some might call it hand washing, but we don't. That would take the fun out of it. Hopefully, by the time they get back our food will be here.

The kids arrive back. Still there is no food to eat. I say to my husband, "Just think, after the long wait, it will taste even better." Our food does arrive finally. I say to my family, "Truly, this is the best salad with grilled chicken I have ever had." In which my six-year-old son replied, "Yeah, that's probably because it was made with such love."

There you have it. This town was so peculiar and kind and loving that even our six-year-old could feel it and identify it. I couldn't have said it better myself.

To wrap up the story, we soon picked up our vehicle and were back on the road after our magical delay. But one day when I get to heaven, I'll have to ask whether it was really the best salad I ever had, or if I just think it was because of the love that I knew went into making and serving it. That must be why this saying is famous, "The best way to a man's heart is through his stomach." Someone is on to something that food served with "love" is a powerful thing that even a six-year-boy can identify!

We should all be so consumed with loving on others in little ways that people feel what we felt in that little town. It was calming, beautiful, real, and distinct. It was peculiar. I imagine this town is like what God wants us to be. This is how we were designed to be in this world.

The love factor has a powerful symbolic meaning and relevance in our modern faith walk that we need to reclaim. We can reclaim this promise to more readily, more consistently avail ourselves to work in the world as designed by God to be representatives of Christ in love.

You see, as God chose to show love through another (Jesus) to us, we are to now show the love of God through ourselves to others. If we are to truly represent God in the world, we are to follow and do as Jesus did. Jesus sacrificed himself for the love of others; we too are to sacrifice self for the love of others.

Remember in Romans 13:14, "Rather, clothe yourselves with (put on) the Lord Jesus Christ, and do not think about how to gratify the desires of the sinful nature." It doesn't come naturally to want to expose ourselves to the hardships of the world and become vulnerable and sensitive to the needs of the world. We will discuss more of these actions we are required to do in the next chapter. We do this by putting on our 'Jesus jackets' and taking off the ones we ourselves have purchased to wear.

It is through these shared words that I hope Christians will be able to better understand how God designed us for love, and how we can come closer to living this way on a consistent basis.

As we begin to move in the world as Christ, each moment spent loving and serving others adds another thread to the Jesus jacket He is weaving that He wants us to wear all the time. Over time, the Jesus jacket becomes complete, and we want to wear it always. We truly become instruments of reconciliation to right all the wrongs of the world as Jesus was purposed for reconciliation through love. That's not to say we won't have buttons fall off of our 'Jesus jackets', or we won't get holes in our 'Jesus jackets'! But, if we all better came to understand the heart and love of Jesus through committed love and service towards others, well, I can't even begin to imagine how many more would come to know this Jesus, our friend. Watch out world!

Let's now take a look at the scripture treasure that God has for us to help us understand and relate this defining love characteristic within our modern faith walk.

In the scriptures, Jesus brings us to the love factor as a crucial component, if not the most relevant one that affects how we move in this world for God. Every task, every deed and every mission, no matter how small or how large, is to start from, is sustained in and completed through love.

Let us contemplate the love factor in and through Jesus in the Bible story found in the gospels of Matthew and Mark where a lot of questions are being thrown at Jesus to test him. One of the Pharisees, an expert in the law then asks Jesus, "Teacher, which is the greatest commandment in the Law?" (Matthew 22:36). But before we seek the answer Jesus gives, let's think about a few things. Do we really understand the question at hand in the context it was asked long ago?

If I may be allowed to reword the question as we might ask today, we could ask it this way, "Teacher, which command, rule, precept or order is the most important of all the ones given, from the first Ten Commandments spoken by God to the last of the other 613 rules documented in the OT by Moses from God?"

We are a Peculiar People Defined by Love 71

As we contemplate the question, let's also contemplate the answer. Somehow I come to expect that the answer Jesus will give will be one of the Ten Commandments. After all the Ten Commandments were the fundamental principles or morals directly spoken by God to Moses for His people. Wouldn't you expect the answer to be one of the Ten Commandments?

So, let's check out Jesus' answer to Mr. Smarty Pants Pharisee. His response is this, "'Love the Lord your God with all your heart and with all your soul and with all your mind' (Deuteronomy 6:5). This is the first and greatest commandment. And the second is like it: 'Love your neighbor as yourself'" (Leviticus 19:18) (Matthew 22:36-39). Last I checked these two commandments spoken by Jesus are not on the list of Ten Commandments. Why wouldn't Jesus quote from the Ten Commandments as they were written or known, and choose some "rule" instead of the "supreme law?" Let's review the Ten Commandments from Exodus 20:3-17, shall we?

1. "You shall have no other gods before me.

2. You shall not make for yourself an idol in the form of anything in heaven above or on the earth beneath or in the waters below. You shall not bow down to them or worship them; for I, the LORD your God, am a jealous God, punishing the children for the sin of the fathers to the third and fourth generation of those who hate me, but showing love to a thousand {generations} of those who love me and keep my commandments.

3. You shall not misuse the name of the LORD your God, for the LORD will not hold anyone guiltless who misuses his name.

4. Remember the Sabbath day by keeping it holy. Six days you shall labor and do all your work, but the seventh day is a Sabbath to the LORD your God. On it you shall not do any work, neither you, nor your son or daughter, nor your manservant or maidservant, nor your animals, nor the alien within your gates. For in six days the LORD made the heavens and the earth, the sea, and all that is in them, but he rested on the seventh day. Therefore the LORD blessed the Sabbath day and made it holy.

5. Honor your father and your mother, so that you may live long in the land the LORD your God is giving you.

6. You shall not murder.

7. You shall not commit adultery.

8. You shall not steal.

9. You shall not give false testimony against your neighbor.

10. You shall not covet your neighbor's house. You shall not covet your neighbor's wife, or his manservant or maidservant, his ox or donkey, or anything that belongs to your neighbor."

Nowhere are these two things Jesus tells us in the list of the Ten Commandments, yet the Son of God says these two things are the most important principals in which to live by!

When we think about this, there should be a grumbling in our spirit, or a great logical concern wondering why Jesus said these two things. It's as if we were driving on a road to Disney World,

We are a Peculiar People Defined by Love   73

having been there before. We know the way. We know how to get there. We don't even need a map. Yet, when we get to 30 miles out from our planned destination there is a huge sign over the highway that says, "Disney World is 613 miles in the opposite direction. Do a u-turn and go the other way." Wouldn't you stop the car and ask, "How could this be?"

We must ask ourselves, why Jesus answered as He did. Why didn't He answer with one of the Ten Commandments? And if these two laws are so important, why didn't God speak them in the original list with the other underlying principals of our covenant relationship?   Why are these cherished scriptures, words summarized and spoken together, only at this time, for the first time and by Jesus, the Son of God?

Biblical scholars suggest that what Jesus is doing is for the first time summarizing the Ten Commandments into two groups. As described by Holman in his Illustrated Bible Dictionary, that the original Ten Commandments can be "interpreted legitimately as a Bill of Rights, perhaps the world's first Bill of Rights. Yet unlike modern bills of rights, this document seeks not to secure my rights, but to protect the rights of others." "The first four statements protect the rights of the covenant Lord; the last six protect the rights of the covenant community."

So, as Tina Turner would sing, "What's love got to do with it?" What I see is that Jesus has to bring us back to the Ten Commandments being about love. Somewhere along the way God's people lost the love factor for which the Ten Commandments and all other laws were created. When we read the account of the giving of the Ten Commandments, we so often focus on the commandments that we overlook the crucial statement God starts with in Exodus 20:2. The Lord begins the dialogue with, "I am the Lord your God, who brought you out of Egypt, out of the land of slavery." God starts by focusing us on the fact that because He loves us, He brought us out of Egypt. Because He loves us, He delivered us from our slavery. "I love you. I want you to show your love for me by living by these principles."

Only what happened? God's people forgot about the love part, didn't they? Living by the principles established by God became about the Law. It became about living a pious life. It became about living a rule-abiding life instead of a life guided by a moral compass to please and honor God with love because He loves us.

I think that is why God had to preface the speaking of the Law with His statement about love. He knew we needed a constant, permanent reminder of why the law was being given, as a choice to abide in because we love Him. Only we forgot anyway (imagine that).

So, we first have the wonderful and beautiful deliverance from our oppression of slavery to Egypt by God. He saved us, bringing us to a place of obedience to the moral law out of love for God. God's design was to have His people abide by the law as a response to His salvation. The law was not given to become a requirement to abide and therefore, receive salvation.

Then we have the wonderful and beautiful deliverance from our oppression of slavery to sin by God through the sacrifice of Jesus. Jesus not only is the way, but points to the way God designed His people to live, a way of love.

As mentioned, Jesus summarizes the law into two categories. The first four commandments could be categorized as those that when we abide by them we demonstrate our love for God, and the rest pertain to how we are to love and treat others.

Jesus brings us back to the defining moment that we are a peculiar people defined by love. Jesus' response to the pious Pharisee redirects His people's focus. Jesus shifts the focus from commitment to a set of rules as a condition for blessings and salvation to a commitment to our God involving our whole being.

Jesus brings us back to the roots of our heritage as we walk in our Christian faith. The heritage designed by God that we receive the gift of salvation, and as a response to that gift, we wholeheartedly respond with love for God and love for others.

When we come to move in the world with a heart motivated by love for God and others, we will come to see and understand God in a profoundly new way. We will fully understand, comprehend and feel what it is like to "Love the Lord your God with all your heart and with all your soul and with all your mind, and love others as yourself" (Matthew 22:37, 39b).

Jesus purposes that we are to love as God designed and as God exposes to each of us in a soup kitchen-like experience. Our love for God flows forth to others for Him like this, "the heart, soul, and mind, are the will, affections, and understanding; or the vital, sensitive, and intellectual faculties. Our love of God must be a sincere love, and not in word and tongue only, as theirs is who say they love him, but their hearts are not with him. It must be a strong love, we must love him in the most intense degree; as we must praise him, so we must love him, "with all that is within us" (Psalm 103:1). It must be a singular and superlative love. We must love him more than anything else. This is the way the stream of our affections must entirely run. The heart must be united to love God, in opposition to a divided heart. All our love is too little to bestow upon him, and therefore all the powers of the soul must be engaged for him, and carried out toward him,"[1] toward Him when we meet Him face to face today in the least of these. "Dear children, let us not love with words or tongue but with actions and in truth," (1 John 3:18) as our forefather Abraham did.

Through our faith in action with the least of these, we are transformed further into a mature place in our faith where we can't help but naturally come to worship and glorify God in all that we do with our transformed merciful hearts. Or, it can be described like this, "The reading of Scripture grows beyond a quiet motion

---

1 http://www.blueletterbible.org/commentaries/comm_view.cfm?AuthorID=4&contentID=1617&commInfo=5&topic=Matthew&ar=Mat_22_36

of religious devotion and (we) rise up into a corporate movement of mercy, justice and humble sharing of the news about God who is Jesus Christ."[1] It's when our focus and heart become about serving God by serving His flock and those that need our mercy, including those who are not His flock.

Oh how I want a heart of mercy like our God! It is in a crucial faith moment that we, a peculiar people defined by love, show the world this love through our actions. It's how God designed us. As described in the Bible "You see that his (Abraham's) faith and his actions were working together, and his faith was made complete by what he did" (James 2:22). When we work in the world we come to live this truth and come to understand this truth that our works complete our faith.

It becomes even clearer when we look to the word root of "made complete" which is the Greek word teleioō which means to carry through completely, to accomplish, finish, or bring to an end. In other words, there is a cause and effect relationship between our faith and our works done in love which results in a deeper, mature, complete or perfect faith.

By having our faith come alive in action, in service to the world, our heart absorbs the very nature of God, this God of mercy. Our faith in action brings about a transformation in our inner beings to relate to God's mercy for the least of these. It's amazing how we are designed to actually get to know God, feel God, and experience God! It is faith that takes on the nature of God, in this case the merciful heart of our God.

God gave me the visual image of the sifting of flour to understand this concept. One sifts flour through a sieve, as God sifts our faith through the sieve of our works. When we understand the reason that some recipes call for sifting we come to understand how God designed our faith walk and how it is very closely tied to our works.

---

[1] Asbury Theological Seminary, Kingdom Tide Reader 2009, "The Kingdom of Heaven is…Already! Not Yet?" pg 7.

We are a Peculiar People Defined by Love

The reason for sifting, as provided by Rose Levy Beranbaum in *The Cake Bible*,[1] is to separate and aerate the flour particles to make them absorb liquids better by de-lumping and smoothing out the texture to make all flour particles consistent so they absorb the water consistently, at the same rate, in the same proportion.

So, our works act as the sieve that sifts our faith flour? Wow! You mean God wants to aerate our faith so that we absorb Him better and absorb our faith better? You bet! Who doesn't need de-lumping and more consistency in our faith walk? It's so amazing how God created this mysterious process of transformation so that we can actually experience the heart of God!

Every work or deed or act of love in the world for God defines us by transforming us. God shows us, tells us, and demonstrates to us that our faith, rooted in love, will be made complete, or fuller, more mature, and more relevant if we work it out. By working it out, we stop limiting our faith because we then allow God to define our faith and who we are.

It's like that 'a-ha moment' when we realize that we just have to get out of the way and let Him do the work. By working out our faith, we are transformed into Christian champions. A Christian champion has faith that not only talks the talk, but walks the walk. Christian champions are Christians empowered by being a peculiar people defined by love, with an understanding of the social implications of our faith, of the Body of Christ to be the hands and feet of Jesus in a hurting world.

It's what some might say is having your faith transformed from a noun into a verb. It's about loving and doing in the world with abandon to liberality, to give without want of getting, to provide help instead of sending help, to work towards understanding the very nature of God by moving among His chosen people, the poor, the hungry, the thirsty, the imprisoned, the naked, the homeless,

---

1 http://www.straightdope.com/columns/read/1635/whats-the-purpose-of-sifting-flour

the hurting, and the unsaved. It's about having our hearts molded into hearts of mercy like the heart of God.

When we, a peculiar people defined by love, are a people with faith that moves us to love as designed in action, and in the places where God designed to fortify and reiterate that love with the least of these, what happens is what I like to describe as the wind-chime effect.

In our modern faith walk we are lacking a connection with our fundamental design to serve the least of these, and in so doing we are like a wind chime hanging in a building (the church). Here we are not able to reach our full potential for producing sounds until we are placed outside the church walls in serving others to have the wind come (the Holy Spirit) and move us so that we yield a beautiful sound that others can hear.

- We are like a Broadway production. We practice and practice, but until we have an audience with whom to share our talents, our work is in vain.
- We are like a pitcher of ice cold tea on a hot summer day. We anticipate being poured into glasses to be consumed, providing relief and quenching thirst.
- We are like the paints on the tip of a paint brush, ready to burst forth our destiny when we meet canvas, to display an image of color and creativity that emanates emotion and life.
- We are a story book on a shelf, waiting to be picked up and opened to come alive through a voice, where we take a child on a journey of imagination to wonderful places unseen.
- We are like a computer program that has yet to be run to calculate algorithms, that will be used in "a biological neural network, in a mechanical device that will deliver electrodes contracting the heart muscles, to regulate the beating of the heart, as a heart monitor.[1]

Let us wait no longer to find relevance and meaning in our modern faith walk. That relevance will be provided in and through the least of these. They remove boulders on the road to Mount Zion when we, a peculiar people defined by love, set out to move in the world!

Let us wait no longer to produce beautiful wind chime sounds out in the open air, to provide relief by quenching thirst, to emanate emotion and life, or to take a child on a journey of imagination to places unseen. Ah, can you hear faint, sweet angelic singing from on high... and they'll know that we're Christians by our love, by our love.[2]

KEY MEMORY VERSES

1. God so loved the world that he gave his one and only Son, that whoever believes in him shall not perish but have eternal life. – John 3:16

2. Rather, clothe yourselves with (put on) the Lord Jesus Christ, and do not think about how to gratify the desires of the sinful nature. – Romans 13:14

3. Dear children, let us not love with words or tongue but with actions and in truth. – 1 John 3:18

---

1 http://en.wikipedia.org/wiki/Algorithm#Computer_algorithms
2 http://www.christianlyricsonline.com/artists/carolyn-arends/theyll-know-we-are-christians.html

QUESTIONS FOR DISCUSSION

1. Discuss how we as believers are designed to be instruments of reconciliation to right all the wrongs of the world like Jesus was purposed for reconciliation through love.

2. Discuss how Jesus fulfilled the law and how this provided the base for the new commandments Jesus commands.

3. Discuss how God's design of how Jesus came to be God's physical presence in the world of God's love for us, and now we Christians are to continue Jesus' work by displaying the love of God to others.

4. Do we know and love God so much that we feel compelled to love in the ways designed? Discuss why or why not?

5. Will you begin to educate yourself on needs in your community and further avail yourself to be used to affect changes for these causes for God's purposes?

6. What if we… _____
   (fill in the blank.)

8

DEFINING MOMENTS: WHAT ARE WE TO "DO" ANYWAY?

What a ride so far! So, God has designed us to experience Him in and through the least of these. As we avail ourselves to be transformed through our encountering Jesus in them, we have our hearts appropriately aligned with a merciful heart like God's. This Godly heart gives us the propensity to love others in a peculiar way.

Through this transforming process, our faith is changed from a noun to a verb. It becomes a faith mobilized and moving in the world. It is faith that flavors the world with a taste of God.

As a peculiar people defined by love, we become the salt that goes into the world to flavor it with a taste of God's love demonstrated through our actions, or what we "do."

But, what exactly are we to "do?" Exactly where, how far, how deep and how wide does God want us to go? Are works what we do with our spiritual gifts? Could random acts of kindness be works? Or should our works be intentional instead of random? Do our works come naturally in the way we live our life, or are they cultivated? Do they just spring forth from our love of mankind, or do we struggle with our sinful selfish nature, and have to work at or choose to have self die every day, if not every moment to keep focused on God and others and not on self?

We really need to search for the Godly meaning of what it is we are to "do." I think we can all agree that if we have a job to do, we better fully understand the job description! So, I present an approach to understanding our Christian job description in three parts, answering the questions of what, how, and why.

In general, *what* is it that we do for God? Do we have specifics we do for God? We may read the Bible, study scriptures and go to church, but what other specifics do we do for the kingdom? How busy are we with the things of this world and our lists of things to do like make breakfast, make lunches, grocery shop, take a shower, drive to work, brush teeth, watch television, read the paper, do homework, give kids bath, play cards, have friends over for dinner or go to a movie?

How much of God's work do we engage our time in? Have we ever inventoried what occupies our time? How much of what we do is for God's glory? Can daily living like making breakfast and reading books be for God's glory? Are they for God's glory? How do we know they are for His glory? What about watching television or spending time surfing the web? Are they for God's glory?

What things do we need to realign with the work of the LORD, and what things do we need to get rid of to free up some time for God specifics? Where can we find the time to adjust our focus so that we can do more of God's work? How do we know if we are doing God's work in all we do?

We must come to evaluate all that we do in a day, moment by moment to make sure that we are selecting building materials that support the construction of the God building. We must come to evaluate whether or not what we do is aligned with kingdom purpose and with the heart of God. All that we do must align with the nature of God displayed in our ordinary daily tasks.

Yes, some tasks are required in our daily living to function in the world, like buying food, preparing it, and eating it. And yes, when these things are done with the heart of God, they bring much joy and glory for the kingdom!

What mother cannot say great things about matching socks and thanking God for the opportunity to serve our families by washing and matching those socks, or by praying over those socks that when they are on the feet of our family they bring guidance unto their path of God's way?

But a lot of the tasks that fill our day are simply a function of being in the world and are not relevant to the work or heart of our God. I would bet right now that the Holy Spirit already brings to mind many daily things we do that are not in alignment with being specific for the purposes of the kingdom of God.

It is not a complicated matter to see the difference, but it is a complicated matter to de-clutter our day of meaningless tasks. We are called to sift through our inventory of daily deeds and determine their meaning in the life of a Christian. When we come to focus on Christ and His ways, we learn to better discern which of our tasks bring glory to the kingdom.

The next question we should ponder is *how* are we to work? One of the main underlying, repeated themes given us in the New Testament is to do as Jesus did, and not just to do what He did, but *how* He did it. In all things, Jesus' actions were aligned with a kingdom perspective. Jesus worked, walked, talked, fished, prayed, led, healed, consoled, washed feet, and died with purpose and intention to affect God's kingdom. I therefore suggest that all of our works no matter how small or big are done with purpose and intent.

It's about learning to walk the walk, not just talk the talk in a lifelong endeavor to align our spirits with the spirit of God. Works for God are not random byproducts of our day with ripple effects for the kingdom. There is a clear picture of what our daily undertakings involve when we look at the following scriptures. All of these scriptures use verbs, which require action, purpose, effort and intention. Let's take a look, shall we?

- "The night is nearly over; the day is almost here. So let us put aside the deeds of darkness and put on the armor of light" (Romans 13:12). God shows us here that at the start of each day choices are to be made. He tells us to wake and to be intentional, laying out two outfits to wear for the day, and making a choice. He tells us to put aside darkness, and put on light.

- "But now you must rid yourselves of all such things as these: anger, rage, malice, slander, and filthy language from your lips. Do not lie to each other, since you have taken off your old self with its practices and have put on the new self, which is being renewed in knowledge in the image of its Creator" (Colossians 3:8-10). It's spring cleaning day every day! We must throw out the junk, take off old self and put on new self. Luckily putting on our new self is a constant renewing from Christ. It is not a one time thing! We are graced with a new start, moment by moment!

- "Therefore, as God's chosen people, holy and dearly loved, clothe yourselves (put on) with compassion, kindness, humility, gentleness and patience" (Colossians 3:12). Not only must we choose to put on the new outfit for ourselves every day, but this scripture gives us details of what to wear. Much like deciding to wear pants or shorts, God instructs us to choose to put on particular things that are the nature of God. When we clothe ourselves in God's character we display him in the world and not us. This is when we become the salt that flavors the world with a taste of God!

- "Rather, clothe yourselves with (put on) the Lord Jesus Christ, and do not think about how to gratify the desires of the sinful nature" (Romans 13:14). This scripture shows that we have choices to make about what our mind thinks about. With the flow of thought, word, and deed we are instructed to first think of things as Jesus would. The WWJD movement comes to mind. Mentally work to focus on Jesus' way, not our way.

- "Surely you heard of him and were taught in him in accordance with the truth that is in Jesus. You were taught, with regard to your former way of life, to put off your old self, which is being corrupted by its deceitful desires; to be made new in the attitude of your minds; and to put on the new self, created to be like God in true righteousness and holiness" (Ephesians 4:21-24). Much like the preceding scripture references, there is instruction with each decision made to yield self and abide in Christ, but this one starts with one key component to lend us the ability to do so, and that is to be taught about Jesus. Where do we learn about Jesus? Ah, not just at church, folks! That is the main lesson of my experience to share with you.

We must avail ourselves and work in the world with the least of these to better understand the heart of Jesus. We must come to know Jesus, not just about Jesus.

- "Therefore, since we are surrounded by such a great cloud of witnesses, let us throw off everything that hinders and the sin that so easily entangles, and let us run with perseverance the race marked out for us. Let us fix our eyes on Jesus, the author and perfecter of our faith, who for the joy set before him endured the cross, scorning its shame, and sat down at the right hand of the throne of God. Consider him who endured such opposition from sinful men, so that you will not grow weary and lose heart" (Hebrews 12:1-3). I'm glad to throw off hindrances, to run the race, and fix my eyes on Jesus! And, let's not miss the promise here that when we do run this race and fix our eyes on Jesus, we will not grow weary or lose heart! Jesus is all the carbohydrates we need to have the fuel to run this race!

- And we must not forget the armor of God, "put on the full armor of God so that you can take your stand against the devil's schemes. For our struggle is not against flesh and blood, but against the rulers, against the authorities, against the powers of this dark world and against the spiritual forces of evil in the heavenly realms. Therefore put on the full armor of God, so that when the day of evil comes, you may be able to stand your ground, and after you have done everything, to stand. Stand firm then, with the belt of truth buckled around your waist, with the breastplate of righteousness in place, and with your feet fitted with the readiness that comes from the gospel of peace. In addition to all this, take up the shield of faith, with which you can extinguish all the flaming arrows of the evil one. Take the helmet of salvation and the sword of the Spirit, which is the word of God. And pray in the Spirit on all occasions with all kinds of prayers and requests. With this in mind, be alert and always keep on praying for all the saints" (Ephesians 6:10-18). Action verbs abound within the armor of God like put on, take up, struggle, buckle, extinguish, pray and stay alert. These preparations for battle are different from the others though. The previous warnings and work focus on the battle with self, but this warning shows we must purposefully prepare for battle from external forces of evil.

Within these scriptures, these warnings and choices show us how to go about our works; with purpose and a conscious undertaking. The bottom line is clearly laid out that there is an inherent sacrifice to be made in order to do works for God. As Abraham's defining moment required a sacrifice, the sacrifice of his son, we too must offer a sacrifice, the sacrifice of self. Here is where the battle lays to undertake what it is God will have us do to experience a life of purpose and meaning.

What will we undertake to do? Will we say "No" to the leading of the Holy Spirit, our great counselor, and respond "Yes" to self?

If we say "Yes" to self, it will be at the sacrifice of us fulfilling God's purposes to affect the world around us.

This has kingdom ramifications folks! The enemy gets us so wrapped up in self that we fail to see that our daily intentions have serious kingdom ramifications. The end result of selfishness is lost works for the kingdom of God.

Yes, the LORD sets us apart as holy by transforming us. Yes, the LORD reconciles us to Him through Jesus' body and blood. And, yes, the LORD gives us the Holy Spirit to empower us to live transformed lives, but we have to work at being Christ-like through learning to deny self, flesh and temptation from the enemy.

It seems so clear through scripture how we are to do works, but it is not easy. It takes discipline to learn to deny the flesh its sinful nature to have it our way. I mean, who cannot relate to this passage when Paul is writing to the Romans, "And I know that nothing good lives in me, that is, in my sinful nature. I want to do what is right, but I can't. I want to do what is good, but I don't. I don't want to do what is wrong, but I do it anyway. But if I do what I don't want to do, I am not really the one doing wrong; it is sin living in me that does it. I have discovered this principle of life—that when I want to do what is right, I inevitably do what is wrong. I love God's law with all my heart. But there is another power within me that is at war with my mind. This power makes me a slave to the sin that is still within me" (Romans 7:18-23).

Our next question is to ask *why* we do what we do. But let's first be clear why *not!* We do *not* do any deed or works as a condition to receiving blessings or love from God.

We are right back to the list of the Ten Commandments that God sets forth. We abide by all He asks of us because of who He is. We abide by all He asks because of what He did and does for us. We are right back to the point that we are a peculiar people defined by love. We do all things out of love for God and others.

If I may use the example of a water pitcher to reason through why we do what we do. The pitcher starts out empty. Then as we receive the many blessings from God, those blessings fill the pitcher with water. When the pitcher is full, it overflows to its surrounding area. The water seeps into its new surroundings. It dampens things. It changes things. It changes the consistency of things.

That, my dear friends, is the evidence of our faith, the affect we have around us. We need to be able to fully comprehend that why we do deeds is because our good deeds or works are evidence of our faith. They bring glory to God and further the Kingdom of God! Our faith works produce fruit, if you will, for the Kingdom of God.

We are so blessed to serve a God who arranges it so that by believing in His son, Jesus, we are empowered by the Holy Spirit to have fruit in our lives. Seems easy enough, right? What's the catch then? I'm glad you asked. The catch is that the Holy Spirit may lead us, but we may not always follow the leadings of the Holy Spirit.

The disciple, John, summarizes this point so beautifully in his writing, "Abide in me, and I in you. As the branch cannot bear fruit of itself, except it abide in the vine: no more can ye, except ye abide in me" (John 15:4 KJV).

It is only by the power of the Holy Spirit that we have fruit in our lives. But, we have to do our part in love. God gives us the choice to follow the leadings of the Holy Spirit or not. When we do not follow the Holy Spirit, we do not have fruit in our lives. When we do follow the Holy Spirit, we have fruit in our lives.

OK, so can we talk about this fruit thing then? What is fruit of the vine? Let's just call this the end product of anything we do, by any means we must employ to further the kingdom of God. I will break down these fruits for the Kingdom of God into two categories. The categories are fruits we may see, the other are fruits that we may not see.

For the fruits we may see, let's use the example of when we throw a rock into a calm lake. You throw a rock, or do an act of kindness for someone. The rock meets the water and immediately you see rings rippling, emanating from where the rock was thrown.

These are our works for the kingdom that produce an immediate effect that we can literally see or feel or hear. They have a direct effect, and we get direct feedback. I sure like these types of fruit. They are encouraging and make our work seem relevant.

Then there are the fruits of our labor that we will never know about. These are not rocks thrown in the lake, but perhaps things as small as a cracker crumb that lands in the lake. The ripple the crumb makes is so small that we just can't see it. To quote Scott Adams, "Every act creates a ripple with no logical end." You never know when a seemingly simple look or touch or smile will be long remembered.

I long remember a person standing behind me at my sister's funeral (yes, the one that was Jill when we played Charlie's Angels), some eighteen years ago and what she did. As we bowed our heads in prayer at the grave site, my long hair fell forward over my shoulder, and this woman reached forward from behind me and ever so gently swept some of the hair from my face and tucked it behind my right ear.

I can't even begin to explain why that moment is burned into my memory and how it made me feel, but it's there. In that moment, I felt so loved. Yes, I one day saw this woman, and told her that I cherished that moment (which of course was so small in her daily living that she didn't remember it).

But unlike this woman who was told what a beautiful thing she did, in most cases, there is no way for us to ever know if some small act of love, service or kindness will produce fruit for the kingdom. The fact of the matter is that there is probably more fruit that we don't know about than we do.

It is just this kind of ambiguity that the enemy feeds off. I believe the enemy uses this randomness factor against us. He makes it seem like we will never know about our works, so we are off the hook. Ambiguity is another player on the enemy's team that we need to know about. His plays will have us believing that there is no accountability for the things we do, so why do them?

Or he'll make it seem like we are working uphill with a wagon full of boulders on our way to Mount Zion that is exhausting. He'll make it feel like doing kind and loving things is a bottomless pit of quick sand that sucks the life out of us (yes, I can be a bit dramatic).

He'll steal the joy of giving by convincing us there is no fruit of our works, and that we give in vain. He may even persuade us into thinking that we are doing good things to earn God's love (which we know can't be earned). Oh, the deceit and lies are great!

But, fear not. Let us ask ourselves, so, how do we know if anything we do produces fruit for the kingdom? And if we don't know, can we just then go about our day and merely hope that what we do will produce some fruit? Does it matter to us if our works are seemingly random or not? Are they random? If there is randomness in our daily living, is there still accountability? Does accountability matter to you?

The real question is does accountability matter to our God? Oh, does it ever. God is a God of accountability on Judgment Day. God has a clear plan for what it is we are to do. Our works are to glorify God and to further His kingdom and are not random, not ever. So, can we, or how do we reconcile this random ripple factor and our accountability with God's plan for our life and working out our faith?

I believe that God expects us to work at our lives and daily moments by being intentional even when we are unintentional in all that we do, in every moment, in every thought, in every word, in every act. Clear as mud; intentional even when we are unintentional?

I believe that the understanding or clarification of how our seemingly random works are actually accountable to God, and therefore not random, lies in the heart of the matter. It is when our heart and soul are aligned with the Holy Spirit that our faith

What are We to "Do" Anyway?

becomes evident as we move, walk, think, work, eat, sleep, wake, dress, ponder, and seek the ways of the Holy Spirit that our works are not random at all. They are for the glory of God.

When we abide in obedience to the leading of the Holy Spirit, we are in line with working with the right intent so that all we do, even random acts or byproducts of our day, are for God's glory.

It's when we act, think, and make decisions to do things or not do things outside of the guidance of the Holy Spirit that they become useless works and will not produce fruit for God.

The key to maintaining meaning and faith in our daily living and works for the glory of God is to learn to walk in the ways of the Holy Spirit. We must obsess with Godly thoughts and ways.

I love this quote by Henry David Thoreau, "As a single footstep will not make a path on the earth, so a single thought will not make a pathway in the mind. To make a deep physical path, we walk again and again. To make a deep mental path, we must think over and over the kind of thoughts we wish to dominate our lives."

It is only by meditating on God and His ways that we will wear a pathway in our mind that leads to an abiding spirit from thought to word to deed. This is where we ask ourselves, what if we were faithful in listening to the leading of the Holy Spirit every day, in every way, in every moment? What if we moved in the direction of doing a little bit more intentional good today than we did yesterday, every day?

So, let's summarize what it is, how it is, and why it is we are to "do" things as Christians. What we do are things that glorify God and further the Kingdom of God. How we do things is with purpose, intent, effort and action according to the Holy Spirit and God's will. We accomplish these things by learning to deny self and abide in the leadings of the Holy Spirit. Why we do things is because we love God and others.

When we allow ourselves to be defined by these characteristics of our faith, we come to live in the full glory of our Godly character. It's living in our Godly understanding and our Godly wisdom. It's how we proceed moment by moment with a focus on God's will and ways. It is the sum of who we are, yet defined moment by moment in every decision or action, or lack thereof.

When we allow ourselves to move in this way in the world, it's like every little thing completed for God's glory can be chalked up with a tick mark on the board of life. I get a visual of the angels up in heaven chalking up another one for God, and the whole team of angels jumping up and down, yelling, "Woo-Hoo," hands Rocky Balboa style over their heads, pumping the air. Let us rejoice in each small victory every day when an act or deed or thing is done for God's glory! It is this kind of focus that will give more relevance to all that we do for Christ!

As our heart is transformed into the heart of God we will come to say, "Yes, I will do it God's way, not my way. Yes, I will give up two hours of television a week to mentor a child. Yes, I will sacrifice my time for shopping to serve lunch to homeless veterans once a week," and on and on.

Which of these events will you choose? A trumpet sounds each time in heaven with angels looking on, several of them tugging at the majestic robe of their "Daddy" (Abba Father) while He is busily attending to the universe, the angels repeatedly tugging and saying, "Daddy look, Daddy look, Daddy look." He looks down at what the angels are looking at, and they say, "Daddy isn't it beautiful? Look, your servant just said yes to the Holy Spirit and is stopping in the grocery store to ask that crying lady if she is OK, and, look at the marvelous light emanating from her as she walks over. It's so wonderful!" And Abba responds, "Yes, it is wonderful," with a warm content feeling in His being and a peaceful smile on His face.

In the other story what happens is... nothing. That is nothing on the earth side. "No," is said to the Holy Spirit leading to go over to the crying woman, for there is no time. "Besides, she might think I'm crazy to ask a stranger if she is OK. I'm sure she doesn't want me in her business. She might be embarrassed that I noticed she is crying."

On the heaven side, the angels block Daddy as He walks over to see what is going on, they implore, "No, Daddy, don't look." As He looks down, His being groans in agony at the grief of a woman crying and lonely, and at His servant that chose self over God's need to have someone care for her in a word and in a moment. The angels' tears run down their faces as they look beyond their master's shoulder at earth, and on earth it begins to rain. Every decision has kingdom ramifications and God does take notice. Oh how I want a heart like God's, don't you?

We have been given the freedom to choose to act or not as God has called us. All we have to do is move in the world for God. I know, easier said than done.

Do not be overwhelmed. The more we do it God's way, the easier it becomes. This is because the more we serve others, the more hurt we see, the more oppression we come to identify, and the more the unbalance of the world becomes apparent and grabs a hold of our heart. With each passing experience of the world's ailments grabbing our heart like it did Jesus', the self dies a little more. The focus is shifted from us to them. We absorb more of God's way, see more of God's nature and take on more of God's nature.

We are exposed to the heart of God when we are moving in the world, and it becomes increasingly difficult to say "yes" to selfishness when you see with the heart of God. We are constantly moved closer to who we are meant to be in Christ, and further away from who we were before we believed in Him.

We have much to do for God! Isn't it great? I say who has time for the things of this world? Say it with me out loud right now as you read this, "Who has time for the things of this world?" This is a phrase we need to recite daily! We have things to do for God! For we can do all things through Christ who strengthens us! (Philippians 4:13 NKJV). That's not some things, dear friend, that's all things!

Key Memory Verses

1. Therefore, as God's chosen people, holy and dearly loved, clothe yourselves (put on) with compassion, kindness, humility, gentleness and patience. – Colossians 3:12

2. Rather, clothe yourselves with (put on) the Lord Jesus Christ, and do not think about how to gratify the desires of the sinful nature. – Romans 13:14

3. Therefore, since we are surrounded by such a great cloud of witnesses, let us throw off everything that hinders and the sin that so easily entangles, and let us run with perseverance the race marked out for us. Let us fix our eyes on Jesus. – Hebrews 12:1-2a

4. Abide in me, and I in you. As the branch cannot bear fruit of itself, except it abide in the vine; no more can ye, except ye abide in me. – John 15:4 KJV

5. For we can do all things through Christ who strengthens us. – Philippians 4:13 (NKJV)

Questions for Discussion

1. Do you experience joy in the mundane tasks of the day to proclaim glory for God, or do you let the enemy deceive you into thinking that they go unnoticed and unappreciated without any impact on the kingdom of God?

2. Spring cleaning time! Take a personal inventory of what things fill your day and evaluate which things are in line with God's work and which things are not. What things need to be added for God's glory? Prioritize which items need to be immediately thrown into the trash and do it! De-junk your life!

3. Discuss areas of deceit the enemy uses to move and keep God's people focused on self instead of others and God. Consider cultural influences, movies, books, main stream media, radio, advertising, and others.

4. Discuss your understanding of the three main questions we should be asking and should be able to answer about our work or deeds for God's kingdom 1) What are we to do? 2) How are we to do them? and 3) Why are we to do them?

9

The Challenge

I suspect many of you may be where I was before I served in the soup kitchen. I also suspect that some of you have served in such humbling roles and places and have experienced what I'm about to explain.

Much of the challenge before us in our modern Christian walk goes back to our defining moments rooted in our Christian heritage. We are back to the stories of the exodus of God's people from slavery in Egypt and the Red Sea experience. Before we can move forward to take the challenge before us to be all that God has called us to be, we need to know where we are.

Where are you in the journey like our forefathers? Are you waiting to be delivered from slavery in Egypt? Are you camping on the shore by the Red Sea? Have you walked through the Red Sea yet?

The soup kitchen experience was my place where I walked across the Red Sea to arrive on the other side as a more mature Christian. I arrived with this new awe and wonder of this God we serve. I arrived with new zeal, but also new questions that we all should be asking.

We are pressed to ask, "Works where and what?" How do you know you are doing the right works? Can there be wrong works? Are you doing enough works? How do you know if your works are in line with God's will and benefit His kingdom?

Are you sure that all that you do brings glory to God. How do you know? Does it matter where you do works for God? What I learned in the soup kitchen is that it does matter where you serve in order for your faith to mature and to become what God intended.

However, there is a growth process to follow. I'm not suggesting that we all arrive at this mature faith with full, deep, wide roots in one growing season. Anyone who has ever had a bush blown over during a storm because the root system wasn't strong enough to support the height growth of the branches knows what I mean when you see an uprooted bush. It takes many seasons and years to grow into a strong balanced bush.

The fact of the matter is that until I better understood the mission and heart of God for His people by serving in the soup kitchen, my growth was stunted. I was like a plant, rootbound in a pot. I needed to be taken out of the pot and planted in the ground.

Until I came to know and love God as described in the previous chapters, my works were honorable, but incomplete. My works before the soup kitchen were stepping stones to maturity, but I was stuck in my teen years. My works in the church and in the world in general provided water to my roots for growth, but lacked nutrients essential to my further growth.

If I may rehash part of my story I was a faithful servant in the church, utilizing my spiritual gifts in teaching. I thought surely my life and my way of life were having some impact for the kingdom of God.

I mean, I drove around with a Christian fish on my car and a cross hanging from my rear view mirror. I even often wore shirts that had a cross on them, or said something spiritual on them so that people would know I was a Christian. I prayed for people. I did kind things. I went out of my way to bring sick friends food. I worked at being a better parent and a more Godly wife.

I was receptive to the pain and trials I had in my life producing some good to make me better for God's works and ways. I studied the Bible. I was forgiving of trespasses. OK, I lost my temper a few times. OK, maybe it was many times with having children go

The Challenge

through the terrible two's, the trying three's, the frightening four's and the fretful fives!

But I thought I was a walking billboard for God hoping others would catch on that Jesus is my Savior and LORD and He should be theirs too. I surely prayed that others would look at me and think, "I want what she has," not in a covetous way of course, but in some evangelical way.

I believed I was doing pretty well in my faith walk, and I wasn't helping directly with the least of these. As a matter of fact, I thought that one had to be called to do such work, and I certainly hadn't heard a call to do that. I mean I took several of those spiritual gifts tests and none of them said I should serve the least of these.

As a matter of fact, when filling out several of those cards from churches to select places to serve, I never saw the category, serve the least of these. I assumed that unless someone had a special "call" from God to serve the disadvantaged, deprived, lonely, needy, it need not apply to me.

I believed that my feeding those within the church walls indirectly resulted in helping the least of these as Paul referred. My works in the church would build up someone else that had the spiritual gift of working with the needy.

So, are you thinking what I was thinking, that your faith is complete yet you don't serve the least of these? Ah, this is where the enemy is working overtime to get a large percentage of Christians to stay serving within the church walls, and not outside of them.

Part of the challenge of this chapter is to reveal the truth behind what is really expected of us to have perfect faith. Get ready for the ride of your life folks! We come before a great and mighty God that has a plan so intricate and amazing in a few beautiful passages, that they will humble us as we witness the living Word of God in these Biblical truths.

I think one of the clearer moments of lucidity I had was when I knew that God would always meet me where I was. But through the soup kitchen my focus went from a selfish focus on how or where God meets me to actually seeking God and asking, "Where can I meet him?"

So, I can certainly relate to the fact that we may think we are accomplishing God's mission here on earth and fulfilling our Christian destiny, but this message is about a God that has designed our salvation experience. It is very hard to describe, but so available to experience when we meet Him where He is.

This is about seeking God and understanding that He is in the least of these, as written in the chapters about God's design to know Him, and God's design to love Him.

Where this brings us to is that as a peculiar people defined by love, this love moves to works of mercy. Once we understand that God designed us to walk among the least of these, to experience the depths of His being, and to be a peculiar people defined by love, we can only then come to have a heart of mercy. A heart which requires us to go deeper into the pain in the world and to emanate our light as a beacon of hope.

God wants us in the middle of pain and despair. I know, that's not a comfortable place to be, but it is a good place to be! You see, a candle emitting its light in a room with the lights on is nice. Its flicker may catch your eye if you look in its direction. However, compare that to a lighted candle set in a dining room with the lights dimmed. Can you now visualize the flicker of the flame that has turned into a dance?

Now, let's go one more step into the darkness. Envision a lighted candle set in the middle of a room, in the middle of the night, in a cabin, in the woods, with no electricity. Does the candle not illuminate the whole room? It emanates so much further, so much more intensely, so much more vividly!

That is how we want the world to see our flame, with vivid intensity! That is how God designed us to be the light of the world, in the midst of the darkness where we can shine the most light.

The Challenge

General works for God are great, but a very concentrated level of nutrients for our growth is found in works of mercy. Faith is incomplete without mercy and action for the plight of those less fortunate. That incomplete faith is rootbound faith.

"What good is it, my brothers, if a man claims to have faith but has no deeds? Can such faith save him? Suppose a brother or sister is without clothes and daily food. If one of you says to him, "Go, I wish you well; keep warm and well fed," but does nothing about his physical needs, what good is it? In the same way, faith by itself, if it is not accompanied by action, is dead" (James 2:14-17).

Our faith without service in the world for the least of these is not yet the faith that God designed for us. I submit that perhaps it's because we have limited God and haven't let go of demanding that He meet us where we are, instead of going and meeting Him where He is. Then and only then can we rise to the challenge to grow in our faith to a mature faith that is pure and faultless.

"Religion that God our Father accepts as pure and faultless is this: to look after orphans and widows in their distress and to keep oneself from being polluted by the world" (James 1:27). God shows that the design of our faith focus or our mercy works are for the least of these.

Focusing on the least of these is like receiving an inoculation from the diseases of this world, the diseases of selfishness, fear, anxiety, and other ailments that inhibit our faith training. Moving in the world to be the light in the darkness makes you immune to the diseases of the world. It's only logical, as many, like UNICEF, are working to get childhood vaccines to children all over the world to prevent 2 million deaths every year."[1]

Wouldn't we go to the least of these for this inoculation from the diseases of the world if we could? Of course, but the enemy is working to stop the distribution of this immunization by

---

[1] http://www.america.gov/st/scitech-english/2009/April/20090430135850CMretroP0.8866236.html

blocking the message of God's mission for His people. This results in religion or faith that lacks relevance in our modern faith walk.

Let us run to the darkness to have our light shine forth! Oh what a promise from God in these scriptures, how to keep Godly focus and not worldly focus. Faith is alive and moving and in action for the least of these. Our faith is like a tree, it is alive, transforming, growing, changing, and forever reaching upward.

It's so amazing and mysterious how God has designed our faith to become action, and how that action morphs us into Christian champions with mature faith! If that isn't reason enough to go into the world where the darkness is and linger, I don't know what is, dear reader!

Perhaps you are one of the many Christian church mice running around soup kitchens all over the country (or serve in many other loving ways with the least of these), and you have experienced our God in these radically new-old ways. If you are, then please, use this book to share what you have experienced to engage more people in the heart of the matter at hand.

Now I know many of you serve with a true servant's heart for only the Glory of God and you hold strong to the scripture that says, "Be careful not to do your 'acts of righteousness' before men, to be seen by them. If you do, you will have no reward from your Father in heaven. So when you give to the needy, do not announce it with trumpets, as the hypocrites do in the synagogues and on the streets, to be honored by men. I tell you the truth they have received their reward in full. But when you give to the needy, do not let your left hand know what your right hand is doing, so that your giving may be in secret. Then your Father, who sees what is done in secret, will reward you" (Matthew 6:1-4).

OK, so many of you are opposed to having others know about your good works because this scripture might lead you to believe that works claimed for God and spoken of are self righteous acts and would then have no reward in heaven.

The Challenge

I understand that completely and have had to reconcile through this and how it fits in my soup kitchen experience, and even writing this book. It sure seems to indicate to keep our good works a secret, doesn't it? So, let's work through this together, shall we?

If we look at a few key words throughout this verse, we get a message regarding the topic of the purpose or intent of the works. Jesus is referencing doing works with the purpose of being seen doing them, proclaiming them, hoping to be honored because of them, and compares those people to hypocrites.

If you are a church mouse serving in a soup kitchen and are worried that if you tell people you are serving in a soup kitchen that God's glory is somehow diminished, then it is impossible for this scripture to reference you.

Just being concerned shows the heart of the matter that you have a servant's heart, and not the heart of a hypocrite. Jesus is saying that if a person's purpose or intent in doing good works is for selfish reasons to make themselves look good, then, yes, there is a major problem and that does not glorify God. If this is your thinking, one should keep these works a secret.

However, if we are abiding in the spirit and serving the least of these as Jesus would, then there is no issue here. Any other interpretation of this is the deceit of the enemy to hide your light under a basket.

The best way I was able to reconcile this and to be comfortable to move forward to share my good works with others was to focus on one of the key missions of God laid forth throughout the Bible. We, as kingdom representatives in the world, are to proclaim God's love to the world.

One of the ways we do this is by our acts of service, and letting the world know we do these things because of the love God has for us, and that we have for all of mankind! We are not talking about hiding our light under a basket anymore. We are talking about setting our light on a lamp stand for all to see. "So that our good deeds shine out for all to see so that everyone will praise your heavenly Father" (Matthew 5:15-16).

So, what I am asking of those of you that I honor and respect, that serve in silence for the glory of God, share the experience! Humbly proclaim your good works for the glory of God! Think about it! What if...what if all 2.1 billion Christians[1] in the world all did only one act per week and proclaimed it in the name of love, for the glory of God? Do you think the world would take notice? Do you think people would begin to ask us who is this God in whom we claim these acts of love ?

The most important suggestion I can give is to be a mentor and a bridge. Open up dialog in your community regarding where you serve. Ask people to come with you once in a while. Post a note in your church bulletin about where you serve and ask if others want to try it with you.

I have found many people that have wanted to try serving in different places, but they were afraid to go alone. I was too, so I took my husband with me to serve in the soup kitchen. Let's not go alone! Take someone with you. Let's not forget that Jesus often sent His disciples out two by two!

As for those of you whom this part of God's mission has lain dormant in your modern faith walk, waiting to be awakened by the sweet kiss of your Prince Jesus (sorry men, but you are His bride too), things are about to get interesting! The challenge is to wake up and engage in the world.

It sounds so easy as the letters fly off my fingers onto the keyboard into the book. Let me assure you, it is not easy. Where did we come to think being a Christian would be easy? But the beauty of the *Soup Kitchen for the Soul* experience is that God has designed and mapped out a treasure hunt to experience Him and His mission for His people in a radically new-old way.

---

1   http://www.america.gov/st/scitech-english/2009/April/20090430135850CMretroP0.8866236.html

The Challenge

All we have to do is go on the adventure laid out by the treasure map and find the spot marked "X". The "X" factor for you is what? Where do you start to serve in the community for the least of these? I don't know, but I know who does. Our gracious, loving God of relationships.

Take a walk with Him in the garden of the world. He will scoop up your arm in His arm. You will not walk alone, you might even skip along with Him, and you will not walk or skip where He hasn't been. Try something, try anything, and try again and again!

I am again reminded of the story in the gospel of Luke about the rich man and Lazarus, "There was a rich man who was dressed in purple and fine linen and lived in luxury every day. At his gate was laid a beggar named Lazarus, covered with sores and longing to eat what fell from the rich man's table. Even the dogs came and licked his sores" (Luke 16:19-21).

I think in today's Christian American experience, we can certainly relate to the rich man who lived in luxury every day. But, we may not have a beggar at our gate. Some may see beggars on street corners, but often that is our only exposure to our Lazarus.

So, if I may offer a word of practicality regarding the treasure hunt you embark upon. Based on the suburban design of many of the cities in which we live, you may have to go further than your front gate to find your modern day Lazarus. But, don't let that stop you!

Start where your church is already providing funding, and ask what if...what if we delivered help to them and didn't just send it, "Don't just meet the needs, meet the people with the needs!"[2] Choose to meet Jesus face to face to allow the beautiful and wondrous design of reciprocity work within you and those you serve.

---

1   http://www.america.gov/st/scitech-english/2009/April/20090430135850CMretroP0.8866236.html

2   Professor Robert Danielson, Asbury Theological Seminary.

Let me remind you that serving in a soup kitchen isn't for everyone, but the defining moments and the promises of God found in the scriptures that I experienced there are. You can experience them too. Encountering God in radically new-old ways awaits you when you listen to the Holy Spirit and abide in God's way to transform the world around you through committed service and love in the world.

This service and love are the things done with intention, with a fervent undertaking, with purpose for God's glory. God's heart of service and love should occupy our thoughts and actions in every small detail of our lives. It is living a truly transformed life available to God at all times and obedient at all costs because we love our God.

That is a heart like our forefather Abraham who was willing to trust God so much and believe in His love and promises without wavering, that he was willing to sacrifice his son if that is what God asked of him.

I pray we are open to the sacrifice of the time from worldly pursuits and pleasures to be used for God's pursuits instead. It is service and love that by denying self to yield to God's way in our daily battle to align ourselves with the Holy Spirit and abide in the Spirit as often as we can, in as many ways as we can. I am reminded of a great quote by John Wesley, "Do all the good you can, By all the means you can, In all the ways you can, In all the places you can, At all the times you can, To all the people you can, As long as ever you can."

It is service and love that is daily. Yes, it may seem uncomfortable at first to step out in faith to do what is against our nature, our flesh, but that's the point. We must move beyond our comfort level to move into the world for Christ. It's not about us and being comfortable.

It's about others, in particular the least of these and finding or providing them comfort. I promise that it does get easier as God begins to transform our hearts to be more like His everyday. That is the heart of the soup kitchen way to experience God. It will transform you, change you, move you and compel you into a more maturing Christian with treasures beyond any words I can write.

May we all search out to experience God in radically new-old ways, however and wherever it is that God will choose to lead you to reveal these truths to you. Some of you may still be pondering and overwhelmed with where to begin.

I still cannot answer that for you, but can offer scripture that may lead you to a heart to start. Let us mull it over with God. He has more promises waiting for you to claim in your modern faith walk that will make life and faith seem more relevant in the world in which we live.

God promises believers that, "You will receive power when the Holy Spirit comes on you; and you will be my witnesses in Jerusalem, and in all Judea and Samaria, and to the ends of the earth" (Acts 1:8). Here is the place marked "Start Here" on your map, your Jerusalem, or your home town. Here is where you should move within first; where you are most comfortable.

Then go to other places like Judea and Samaria, which may be places that require effort to get there, and like Samaria, may be somewhere with people you don't normally associate. You may not even like them. But I bet once you get there, you'll find they are just like the rest of us, and most of the hate and fear in our world is just because of lack of knowledge, heart knowledge.

That it is why it is so important to, "not just meet the needs, but meet the people with the needs."[1] And then, maybe God will call you one day to go some place at the ends earth, far from home, far from your comfort zone.

But, for now, we are talking baby steps. We are talking about serving and loving others through our kindnesses, our tenderhearted mercies, our prayers, and our life actions centered

---

[1] Professor Robert Danielson, Asbury Theological Seminary.
[2] http://www.willowcreek.com/transformation/

on others, not us. "Only when lives, churches, and communities are being transformed by the power of Jesus Christ is God's plan to redeem and restore this world to Him being truly fulfilled."[2] That is one of the key defining moments of the soup kitchen experience!

The promise of your very own soup kitchen experience, whatever it is you find to do in your corner of the world, to affect the world around you for the purposes and plans of God, can be summed up by Peter in his second letter, "In view of all this, make every effort to respond to God's promises. Then your faith will produce a life of moral excellence. A life of moral excellence leads to knowing God better. Knowing God leads to self-control. Self-control leads to patient endurance and patient endurance leads to godliness. Godliness leads to love for other Christians, and finally you will grow to have genuine love for everyone. The more you grow like this the more you will become productive and useful in your knowledge of our Lord Jesus Christ" (2 Peter 1:5-8 NLT).

Somewhere along the way in this description by Peter of our peculiar Christian experience, the defining moment happens when we begin to ask what if... What if we started to change the world right here, right now? What if all 2.1 billion[1] Christians could readily answer the question: "What is it we are supposed to be doing?" And they were doing it! And could reference where in the Bible to do it?

What if a non-believer asked a Christian each day what was our purpose in life, where does our meaning come from, and that Christian could answer with a fervent heart knowledge of God?

What if we were faithful in listening to the leading of the Holy Spirit every day, in every way, in every moment? What if we could get people more out of the box of the four walls of the church to be movers and shakers in the world for the kingdom of God?

---

[1] http://www.adherents.com/Religions_By_Adherents.html, and http://wiki.answers.com/Q/How_many_Christians_are_there_worldwide.

The Challenge

What if we shared this book with one other person (I have to ask because my heart aches for us to do whatever we have to do to help modern faith walkers reconnect with the full missions of God)?

What if we engaged in conversations at our kitchen tables on the topic of asking what if?

What if we all asked ourselves, *what if*...and we all undertook one *what if* thought...and we had a *what if* **serv-o-lution**?

God bless each of you! May you be inspired to engage in new missions for God that bring great glory to God! I pray for all mankind to come to know the real heart of God in today's world. I pray for all Christians to come to experience God in radically new-old ways. I pray for opportunities for you to show God's love moment by moment. I pray for an obedient spirit for you. I pray for God to help you restructure your priorities daily for His purposes. I pray for God to expose hardness in your heart and for it to be removed. I pray for a hedge of protection from the enemy's deceit and lies. I pray for stereotypes to be abolished so you can see with a heart of God where to serve. I pray for world peace. AMEN.

KEY MEMORY VERSES

1. Neither do people light a lamp and put it under a bowl. Instead they put it on its stand, and it gives light to everyone in the house. In the same way, let your light shine before men, that they may see your good deeds and praise your Father in heaven. – Matthew 5:15-16

2. You will receive power when the Holy Spirit comes on you; and you will be my witnesses in Jerusalem, and in all Judea and Samaria, and to the ends of the earth. – Acts 1:8

3. In view of all this, make every effort to respond to God's promises. Then your faith will produce a life of moral excellence. A life of moral excellence leads to knowing God better. Knowing God leads to self-control. Self-control leads to patient endurance and patient endurance leads to godliness. Godliness leads to love for other Christians, and finally you will grow to have genuine love for everyone. The more you grow like this the more you will become productive and useful in your knowledge of our Lord Jesus Christ. – 2 Peter 1:5-8

QUESTIONS FOR DISCUSSION

1. Do feel in today's culture that in being or doing our Christianity that it is easy to "let our light shine before men" or is it easier to "light a lamp and put it under a bowl?" Discuss the reasons for your answer.
2. What if all 2.1 billion Christians[1] in the world all did only one act per week and proclaimed it in the name of love, for the glory of God? Do you think the world would take notice?
3. Can you comfortably and confidently say you believe that you can and should proclaim your good works for God as a humble servant? Why or why not?
4. What if we were faithful in listening to the leadings of the Holy Spirit every day, in every way, in every moment?
5. Do you think if you experienced God as I did in the soup kitchen that you would be a more obedient faithful servant of God more often?

---

1 http://www.adherents.com/Religions_By_Adherents.html, and http://wiki.answers.com/Q/How_many_Christians_are_there_worldwide.

The Challenge

6. Have you experienced the relevance of these defining moments and promises of God in your modern faith walk? Which have you experienced, which have you not?
7. The challenge: What is it that you think God is asking of you to do? Do you have a "feeling" about where you should start to serve or love others as you haven't before? Discuss.
8. Who else do you feel compelled to share this book with? Will you?
9. Pray for all Christians to come to have a renewed experience with the heart of God. Pray for peace. Pray for the lost. Pray for the hungry. Pray for the sick. Pray for the homeless. Pray for the malnourished. Pray for the lonely. Pray for the outcasts. Pray for the imprisoned. Pray for all the hurting, the abandoned and the abused. And also pray for more servants because, "The harvest is plentiful, but the workers are few. Ask the Lord of the harvest, therefore, to send out workers into his harvest field" (Luke 10:2). AMEN.

10

AWARENESS TRAINING

One of my favorite verses has always been Romans 8:28, "And we know that in all things God works for the good of those who love him, who have been called according to his purpose." Before we embark on our journey to go and meet God where He is, let us rest assured that EVERYTHING we have experienced has purpose and meaning. This verse says that ALL THINGS, not some things, not most things, but ALL things dear friend will work for the good!

All of our past trials, sins, tribulations, hardships, wrong turns, bad or dangerous experiences WILL be used for good. All of it can be used as a stepping stone to understand and work in fields of influence for God!

Remember the story of our ancestors at the edge of the Red Sea? They heard a voice say, "Get Moving!" As they looked over their shoulders at the impending doom of the Egyptian army and forward at the impending doom of the deep waters of the Red Sea, they had to ask, "Move? Move where?"

"Ah, that is the question!" as Hamlet would say! The purpose of this chapter is to see where the Holy Spirit leads you, or drags you kickin' and screamin' like I was on my way to the soup kitchen. We must start somewhere, so let's see where that might be for you! OK, if you're going to surf the web, let's use it for God's glory! I have included these suggestions as a place to get started to increase our awareness of some issues that we could be involved in.

This is by no means an exhaustive list. Although I may personally find these websites helpful and useful, it is not my intent to endorse any of these for purposes beyond personal. Many of them have newsletters that you can sign up for to be kept abreast of the current changes and information regarding the topics. I hope you are blessed in this first step to become more aware of the needs of the needy in your home town, your state, your world.

Although I suggest you do read each biographic organization summary provided below, I don't suggest you go to all the websites in one week, or week one. I suggest that you pick one or two topics that interest you from the heart and search out information on them on a global scale. Then work down into your national, state or local level on the key topic.

Ready, set, go!

The Hunger Site   www.thehungersite.org

Click to Give Food (use as homepage/click to give food everyday-no cost)

www.thehungersite.com/clickToGive/home.faces?siteId=1

The Hunger Site was founded to focus the power of the Internet on a specific humanitarian need; the eradication of world hunger. Since its launch in June 1999, the site has established itself as a leader in online activism, helping to feed the world's hungry and food insecure. On average, over 220,000 individuals from around the world visit the site each day to click the yellow "Click Here to Give - it's FREE" button. Its grassroots popularity has been recognized with Web awards in the activism category — the 2000 Cool Site of the Year Award and the People's Voice winner at the 2000 Webby Awards. Since its inception, visitors at The Hunger Site and shoppers at The Hunger Site store have given more than 657 million cups of food.

The staple food funded by clicks at The Hunger Site is paid for by site sponsors and distributed to those in need by Mercy Corps, Feeding America (formerly America's Second Harvest), and Millennium Promise. 100% of sponsor advertising fees goes to our charitable partners. Funds are split between these organizations and go to the aid of hungry people in over 74 countries, including those in Africa, Asia, Eastern Europe, the Middle East, Latin America and North America.

Christian Coalition   www.cc.org

Christian Coalition offers people of faith the vehicle to be actively involved in impacting the issues they care about - from the county courthouse to the halls of Congress.

The Coalition is a political organization, made up of pro-family Americans who care deeply about ensuring that government serves to strengthen and preserve, rather than threaten, our families and our values. To that end, we work continuously to identify, educate and mobilize Christians for effective political action.

Our Mission:

– Represent the pro-family point of view before local councils, school boards, state legislatures and Congress

– Speak out in the public arena and in the media

rain leaders for effective social and political action

– Inform pro-family voters about timely issues and legislation

– Protest anti-Christian bigotry and defend the rights of people of faith

Focus on the Family   www.focusonthefamily.com

To cooperate with the Holy Spirit in sharing the Gospel of Jesus Christ with as many people as possible by nurturing and defending the God-ordained institution of the family and promoting biblical truths worldwide.

Focus on the Family Action   www.citizenlink.org

Focus on the Family Action is a cultural action organization that is completely separate from Focus on the Family, legally. It has been created by separating out of Focus on the Family those activities which constitute lobbying under the IRS code so that they can be expanded in scope. It will provide a platform for informing, inspiring and rallying those who care deeply about the family to greater involvement in the moral, cultural and political issues that threaten our nation.

Feeding America   www.secondharvest.org

(formerly named America's Second Harvest)

Feeding America is the nation's leading domestic hunger-relief charity. Our mission is to feed America's hungry through a nationwide network of member food banks and engage our country in the fight to end hunger.

Each year, the Feeding America network provides food assistance to more than 25 million low-income people facing hunger in the United States, including more than 9 million children and nearly 3 million seniors.

Our network of more than 200 food banks serves all 50 states, the District of Columbia and Puerto Rico. The Feeding America network secures and distributes more than 2 billion pounds of donated food and grocery products annually.

The Feeding America network supports approximately 63,000 local charitable agencies that distribute food directly to Americans in need. Those agencies operate more than 70,000 programs including food pantries, soup kitchens, emergency shelters, after-school programs, Kids Cafes and BackPack Programs.

National Coalition for the Homeless

                             www.nationalhomeless.org

The National Coalition for the Homeless is a national network of people who are currently experiencing or who have experienced homelessness, activists and advocates, community-based and faith-based service providers, and others committed to a single mission. That mission, our common bond, is to end homelessness. We are committed to creating the systemic and attitudinal changes necessary to prevent and end homelessness. At the same time, we work to meet the immediate needs of people who are currently experiencing homelessness or who are at risk of doing so. We take as our first principle of practice that people who are currently experiencing homelessness or have formerly experienced homelessness must be actively involved in all of our work. Toward this end, the National Coalition for the Homeless (NCH) engages in public education, policy advocacy, and grassroots organizing. We focus our work in the following 4 areas: housing justice, economic justice, health care justice, and civil rights.

National Coalition against Domestic Violence

www.ncadv.org

The Mission of the National Coalition Against Domestic Violence (NCADV) is to organize for collective power by advancing transformative work, thinking and leadership of communities and individuals working to end the violence in our lives.

NCADV believes violence against women and children results from the use of force or threat to achieve and maintain control over others in intimate relationships, and from societal abuse of power and domination in the forms of sexism, racism, homophobia, classism, anti-Semitism, able-bodyism, ageism and other oppressions. NCADV recognizes that the abuses of power in society foster battering by perpetuating conditions, which condone violence against women and children. Therefore, it is the mission of NCADV to work for major societal changes necessary to eliminate both personal and societal violence against all women and children.

NCADV's work includes coalition building at the local, state, regional and national levels; support for the provision of community-based, non-violent alternatives - such as safe home and shelter programs - for battered women and their children; public education and technical assistance; policy development and innovative legislation; focus on the leadership of NCADV's caucuses developed to represent the concerns of organizationally under represented groups; and efforts to eradicate social conditions which contribute to violence against women and children.

National Immigration Forum   www.immigrationforum.org

Established in 1982, the National Immigration Forum is the leading immigrant advocacy organization in the country with a mission to advocate for the value of immigrants and immigration to the nation. The Forum uses its communications, advocacy and policy expertise to create a vision, consensus and strategy that leads to a better, more welcoming America – one that treats all newcomers fairly.

Ultimately, our vision is to create US immigration policy that honors our nation's ideals, protects human dignity, reflects our country's economic demands, celebrates family unity and provides opportunities for progress.

League of United Latin American Citizens   www.lulac.org

LULAC is the largest and oldest Hispanic Organization in the United States. LULAC advances the economic condition, educational attainment, political influence, health and civil rights of Hispanic Americans through community-based programs operating at more than 700 LULAC councils nationwide. The organization involves and serves all Hispanic nationality groups.

Historically, LULAC has focused heavily on education, civil rights, and employment for Hispanics. LULAC councils provide more than a million dollars in scholarships to Hispanic students each year, conduct citizenship and voter registration drives, develop low income housing units, conduct youth leadership training programs, and seek to empower the Hispanic community at the local, state and national level.

In addition, the LULAC National Educational Service Centers, LULAC's educational arm, provides counseling services to more than 18,000 Hispanic students per year at sixteen regional centers. SER Jobs for Progress, LULAC's employment arm, provides job skills and literacy training to the Hispanic community through more than forty-eight employment training centers located throughout the United States. The LULAC Corporate Alliance, an advisory board of Fortune 500 companies, fosters stronger partnerships between Corporate America and the Hispanic community.

Charity Navigator   www.charitynavigator.org

Charity Navigator, America's premier independent charity evaluator, works to advance a more efficient and responsive philanthropic marketplace by evaluating the financial health of over 5,400 of America's largest charities.

World Vision International   www.wvi.org

World Vision is an international partnership of Christians whose mission is to follow our Lord and Savior Jesus Christ in working with the poor and oppressed to promote human transformation, seek justice and bear witness to the good news of the Kingdom of God.

Who we are: World Vision is a Christian humanitarian charity organization dedicated to working with children, families, and their communities worldwide to reach their full potential by tackling the causes of poverty and injustice.

Who we serve: We serve close to 100 million people in nearly 100 countries around the world. World Vision serves all people, regardless of religion, race, ethnicity, or gender.

Why we serve: Motivated by our faith in Jesus Christ, we serve alongside the poor and oppressed as a demonstration of God's unconditional love for all people.

Heifer's Mission to End Hunger www.heifer.org

Since 1944, when Heifer first shipped cows to impoverished families, we have known that livestock offer one of the best resources for ending the cycle of chronic hunger and poverty that plagues two-thirds of the planet. Since then, Heifer has helped millions of families with gifts of livestock and training.

Heifer's History: This simple idea of giving families a source of food rather than short-term relief caught on and has continued for over 60 years. Today, millions of families in 128 countries have been given the gifts of self-reliance and hope.

Heifer envisions...A world of communities living together in peace and equitably sharing the resources of a healthy planet.

Heifer's mission is...To work with communities to end hunger and poverty and to care for the earth.

Heifer's strategy is...To "pass on the gift." As people share their animals' offspring with others – along with their knowledge, resources, and skills – an expanding network of hope, dignity, and self-reliance is created that reaches around the globe.

CLOSING WORDS

Well dear loved ones of Christ, time for me to sign off. The message God wanted me to share with you is complete.

It is time for you to leave the nest and go fly on your own. Remember, you may be on your own now, but you are never alone. God is with you always! I leave you in the presence and grace of our great and glorious God that wants you to go and seek Him in the least of these.

God bless you and your loved ones!

Key Memory Verse

1. And we know that in all things God works for the good of those who love him, who have been called according to his purpose. – Romans 8:28

Questions for Discussion

1. Your homework this week is to dabble where the Spirit leads you. What are YOU interested in? Still not sure? List out what difficulties have you or one of your loved ones experienced firsthand? Maybe start there? Do you have a friend that has been in abusive relationship? Has your family been exposed to drug or alcohol addiction? Perhaps you have experienced infertility or troubles with pregnancy? Do you have a relative that went through a period of physical abuse or was raped? Do you have a friend in college that experienced sexual abuse as a child? Perhaps you know of someone that was addicted to pornography? Perhaps you grew up in a low income family and experienced hunger or homelessness first hand? Maybe you have a lot of immigrants living in your area. Seek out what it's like for them by asking questions or reading local articles. Maybe you or a family member has learning disabilities that you had to learn to work with or overcome? The potentials are unlimited once you start to see with the heart of God where He can use you!
2. List out at least three spheres of experience to see where your personal interests may lead you. The first sphere should include difficulties you have personally gone through. The second sphere should include difficulties that you know family or friends have personally

experienced. The third sphere is issues pertinent to your local area (like we have particularly high veteran issues). Others might be issues your local church is affiliated with or where you may have the opportunity to easily volunteer.

3. What are the one or two issues you picked to investigate further this week? Explain what you learned. What are the world statistics? Are the national statistics different than global? Is your state or local statistics the same ratios as the national statistics? If they are different, why do you think that is so? What are some of the causes of the issues? Did anything surprise you in particular about your research?

4. Now, I pray that you don't just ask yourself these question, but get together and ask each other and really discuss: *What if.*

What if... we all absolutely knew what God wants us to do and why and pursued it with conviction?

What if... I shared this message with other Christians?

What if... I could do some small part to change our mindset from being a "come to me" God to being a "go to God" kind of Christian?

What if... we could get people to reconnect with our Christian heritage and the Godly design of our faith walk found in the Bible by getting refocused on feeding and serving others and not on self?

What if... Christians came to ask, not what can God do for me today, but what can I do for God and His kingdom today?

What if.

Appendix A:

SUGGESTED BIBLE STUDY READING GUIDE

WEEK 1

Suggest buying/providing group with a plain spiral bound notebook for journaling and answering questions for class time.

1. Watch Intro Video (9 minutes) Can be found on youtube at http://www.youtube.com/watch?v=Cjp_J-Q1c40
2. Read Forward/Introduction and My Story
3. Review "Discussion Questions", journal Discussion Questions' answers before next class.
4. Select at least one favorite memory verse- work on memorizing this week.

WEEK 2

1. Read Chapter 1
2. Review "Discussion Questions", journal Discussion Questions' answers before next class.
3. Select at least one favorite memory verse- work on memorizing this week.

WEEK 3

1. Read Chapter 2
2. Review "Discussion Questions", journal Discussion Questions' answers before next class.
3. Select at least one favorite memory verse- work on memorizing this week.

Week 4

1. Read Chapter 3
2. Review "Discussion Questions", journal Discussion Questions' answers before next class.
3. Select at least one favorite memory verse- work on memorizing this week.

Week 5

1. Read Chapter 4
2. Review "Discussion Questions", journal Discussion Questions' answers before next class.
3. Select at least one favorite memory verse- work on memorizing this week.

Week 6

1. Read Chapter 5
2. Review "Discussion Questions", journal Discussion Questions' answers before next class.
3. Select at least one favorite memory verse- work on memorizing this week.

Week 7

1. Read Chapter 6
2. Review "Discussion Questions", journal Discussion Questions' answers before next class.
3. Select at least one favorite memory verse- work on memorizing this week.

WEEK 8

1. Read Chapter 7
2. Review "Discussion Questions", journal Discussion Questions' answers before next class.
3. Select at least one favorite memory verse- work on memorizing this week.

WEEK 9

1. Read Chapter 8
2. Review "Discussion Questions", journal Discussion Questions' answers before next class.
3. Select at least one favorite memory verse- work on memorizing this week.

WEEK 10

1. Read Chapter 9
2. Review "Discussion Questions", journal Discussion Questions' answers before next class.
3. Select at least one favorite memory verse- work on memorizing this week.

WEEK 11

1. Read Chapter 10
2. Review "Discussion Questions", journal Discussion Questions' answers before next class.

Scripture Index

Exodus 1:22...................................19
Exodus 6:6-7................................. 20
Exodus 6:7b...................................31
Exodus 10:7...................................21
Exodus 13:8...................................25
Exodus 13:12-13...........................27
Exodus 14:11-12...........................29
Exodus 14:13-14....................30, 33
Exodus 14:25.................................31
Exodus 20:2...................................73
Exodus 20:3-17............................. 71
Exodus 31:13.......................... 42, 46
Leviticus 19:18.............................. 71
Leviticus 20:26............................. 37
Deuteronomy 4:29..........................2
Deuteronomy 6:5..........................71
Psalm 103:1...................................75
Isaiah 57:14-15............................. 54
Isaiah 61:1-2........................... 51, 54
Isaiah 61:1-2a................................62
Matthew 5:15-16............... 104, 109
Matthew 6:1-4............................ 102
Matthew 10:19b-20.............. 40, 46
Matthew 22:36.............................70
Matthew 22:36-39........................71
Matthew 22:37, 39b....................75
Matthew 25:35-40........................53
Matthew 28:18-19................ 41, 46
Luke 4:18...................................... 52
Luke 4:14-21.................................54
Luke 4:17-21.................................51
Luke 4:18-19.................................62
Luke 16..61
Luke 16:19-21........................... 105
John 1:41..44
John 1:43-45................................. 44
John 3:16.................................65, 79
John 8:20.......................................50
John 14:6.................................50, 62
John 15:4.................................88, 94
John 17:18.............................. 60, 63
Acts 1:8...............................107, 109
Romans 5:1...........................23, 25
Romans 7:18-23........................... 87
Romans 13:12...............................83
Romans 13:14...65, 69, 79, 84, 94
1 Corinthians 12:1-2....................43
1 Corinthians 12:4-7....................43
2 Corinthians 4:5-7......................36
Ephesians 4:17-18...................... 46
Ephesians 4:17b-18..................... 42
Ephesians 4:21-24...................... 85
Ephesians 6:10-18.................. 6, 86
Philippians 4:13................... 93, 94
Colossians 1:19-20............... 55, 63
Colossians 3:8-10........................84
Colossians 3:12.................... 84, 94
Hebrews 12:1-2a.......................... 94
Hebrews 12:1-3............................85
James 1:27................................. 101
James 2:14-17........................... 101
James 2:22....................................76
2 Peter 1:5-8.....................108, 110
1 John 2:6......................................55
1 John 3:18...................... 75, 79

The Character of Our Discontent

The Character of Our Discontent grew out of the author's conviction that pastors do not preach enough about the Old Testament. The result is 19 chapters, each of which represents a sermon on an Old Testament character. These sermons are lively, fast paced, and practical yet are rooted in sound scholarship and are examples of the homiletical art.

Along Bible Paths: Summer Devotions

Along Bible Paths: Summer Devotions grew out of the daily devotional e-mail list that Jody Neufeld began in 1999 to encourage others to begin their day with the Lord. Many continue to enjoy these thoughts in their e-mail every weekday morning, or via the Jody's Devotionals blog. This book is a collection organized for the summer. We hope many more will enjoy these in printed form.

Learning and Living Scripture: An Introduction to the Participatory Bible Study Method

Geoffrey Lentz and Henry Neufeld, a pastor and a teacher team up in Learning and Living Scripture to present the Participatory Bible Study Method, an approach to Bible study that is rooted in the conviction that God can and will speak to us in scripture.

Join in this study complete with exercises and discussion questions

EnergionDirect.com
http://www.energiondirect.com

Phone: (850) 525-3916
P. O. Box 841
Gonzalez, FL 32560

More from Energion Publications

Personal Study

The Jesus Paradigm	$17.99
When People Speak for God	$17.99
Holy Smoke, Unholy Fire	$14.99
Not Ashamed of the Gospel	$12.99
Evidence for the Bible	$16.99
Christianity and Secularism	$16.99
What's In A Version?	$12.99
Christian Archy	$9.99
The Character of Our Discontent	$12.99
Who's Afraid of the Old Testament God?	$9.99
The Messiah and His Kingdom to Come: A Biblical Road Map	$19.99 (B&W)
(an EnerPower Press title)	$49.99 (Color)

Christian Living

52 Weeks of Ordinary People – Extraordinary God	$7.99
Along Bible Paths: Summer Devotions	$9.99
Daily Devotions of Ordinary People – Extraordinary God	$19.99
Directed Paths	$7.99
Disciples: Jesus With Us	$7.99
Grief: Finding the Candle of Light	$8.99
I Want to Pray	$7.99

Bible Study for Groups

Leraning and Living Scripture	$12.99
To the Hebrews: A Participatory Study Guide	$9.99
Revelation: A Participatory Study Guide	$9.99
The Gospel According to St. Luke: A Participatory Study Guide	$8.99
Identifying Your Gifts and Service: Small Group Edition	$12.99
Consider Christianity, Volume I & II Study Guides	$7.99 each

Politics

Preserving Democracy (Hardcover)	$29.99

Fiction

Megabelt	$12.99
Tales from Jevlir: Oddballs (an Enzar Empire Press title)	$7.99

Generous Quantity Discounts Available   Dealer Inquiries Welcome

Energion Publications
P.O. Box 841
Gonzalez, FL 32560
Website: http://energionpubs.com
Phone: (850) 525-3916

www.ingramcontent.com/pod-product-compliance
Lightning Source LLC
LaVergne TN
LVHW011203080426
835508LV00007B/579